LEGALIZING DRUGS

Other Books in the At Issue Series:

LEGALIZING DRUGS

Louise I. Gerdes, *Book Editor*

Bonnie Szumski, *Editorial Director*
Scott Barbour, *Managing Editor*

An Opposing Viewpoints® Series

Greenhaven Press, Inc.
San Diego, California

Library of Congress Cataloging-in-Publication Data

Legalizing drugs / Louise I. Gerdes, book editor.
    p.   cm. — (At issue)
    Includes bibliographical references and index.
    ISBN 0-7377-0662-7 (hardbound : alk. paper) —
ISBN 0-7377-0661-9 (pbk. : alk. paper)
    1. Drug legalization—United States. 2. Drug abuse—United
States. I. Gerdes, Louise I. II. At issue (San Diego, Calif.)

HV5825 .L439 2001
364.1'77'0973—dc21
                                                        00-065414
                                                             CIP

© 2001 by Greenhaven Press, Inc., PO Box 289009,
San Diego, CA 92198-9009

Printed in the U.S.A.

Table of Contents

Introduction

The prohibition of drugs is a relatively recent phenomenon in the history of the United States. During the nineteenth century, the federal government applied a laissez-faire philosophy to drugs and asserted no control over their manufacture or consumption. Americans interpreted the U.S. Constitution strictly, believing that the federal government had limited powers and should leave the passage and enforcement of most laws to the states. As a result of this "hands off" philosophy, the companies that manufactured and sold addictive drugs were not regulated.

By the beginning of the twentieth century, however, many Americans had become addicted to drugs. Since the 1850s, morphine had been used not only as an anesthetic for use during surgery, but as a routine pain killer. Morphine use was particularly common among Civil War veterans who had received the drug during and after surgery. Many continued to use morphine for chronic severe pain caused by war injuries. By 1880, so many veterans were addicted to morphine that the press referred to morphine addiction as the *soldier's disease*.

Yet Civil War soldiers were not the only drug addicts. At the turn of the century, many middle-aged white women were addicted to drugs. Physicians who were not aware of the dangers of addiction prescribed opium or morphine for such common conditions as menstrual cramps, anxiety, and insomnia. Salesmen roamed the countryside selling potions and elixirs containing alcohol and narcotics such as morphine, cocaine, and opium. These salesmen claimed that their patent medicines could cure diseases ranging from the common cold to tuberculosis. Americans could even obtain these medicines from mail order catalogues.

Because companies were not required to disclose their contents, consumers were often unaware that they were using narcotics. Some of these preparations contained as much as 50 percent morphine, but other powerful drugs often were included.

Sometimes, people used drugs whose dangerous qualities were poorly understood. For example, heroin was considered a nonaddictive treatment for morphine addiction and alcoholism. And from its development in 1886 until 1903, Coca-Cola contained cocaine and was marketed as a "brain and nerve tonic" in drugstores. The availability of these drugs led to a rise in addiction in America.

At the end of the nineteenth century, however, a reforming spirit was evident in the nation. This new attitude led some to believe that addiction to drugs, too, should be addressed through legislative action. The first federal law passed in response to drugs was the Pure Food and Drug Act of 1906. The law not only required that manufacturers list the contents of patent medicines that included morphine, cocaine, opium, or chloral hydrate, but also prohibited manufacturers from making false claims about the benefits of taking these products. Because most companies could not prove the effectiveness of these "medicines," the law led to the demise of the patent medicine industry. However, the Act did not address the use of these drugs by consumers.

Despite a drop in drug addiction following the restriction on patent medicines, the federal government decided to do more to discourage the use of narcotics. In 1914, Congress passed the Harrison Tax Act, which required that doctors pay a yearly tax of one dollar, which allowed them to prescribe drugs containing opium or coca products as long as they followed the statute's guidelines. Although others could buy the drugs for nonmedical uses, the tax on such transactions was set high enough to either discourage purchase of the drugs or to force buyers to evade the tax, in effect criminalizing their use. Enforcement of the Harrison Tax Act was at first assigned to the Internal Revenue Service, but in 1930 the Bureau of Narcotics was established for this purpose.

Not long after the formation of the Bureau of Narcotics, the focus of drug enforcement efforts again shifted. Addicts were now seen as criminals, whether or not they had paid their taxes. According to law professor Charles Whitebread, "The existence of this separate agency anxious to fulfill its role as crusader against the evils of narcotics has done as much as any single factor to influence the course of drug regulation from 1930 to 1970. . . . [T]he existence of a separate bureau having responsibility only for narcotics enforcement and for educating the public on drug problems inevitably led to a particularly prosecutorial view of the narcotic's addict."

The first Commissioner of the Federal Bureau of Narcotics, Harry Anslinger, saw his effort to wipe out addiction as a crusade. His first target, however, was not chemically a narcotic at all; it was marijuana. Again, the federal effort used taxes as its primary tool. The Marijuana Tax Act of 1937 levied taxes on marijuana dealers and a transfer tax on marijuana sales.

Commissioner Anslinger was convinced, as he noted during Congressional hearings, that "marijuana is an addictive drug, which produces in its users insanity, criminality, and death." After Anslinger's appointment to the Bureau of Narcotics, he launched a misinformation campaign against marijuana, enrolling the services of Hollywood and several tabloid newspapers. Exaggerated accounts of the criminal behavior of those who used marijuana became common. As reports of the dangers of using marijuana spread, Anslinger's position against marijuana gained credibility. The Assistant General Counsel for the Department of the Treasury, Clinton Hester, affirmed that the drug's eventual effect on the user "is deadly." Moreover, a *Washington Times* editorial published before the first hearing on the issue argued: "The fatal marijuana cigarette must be recognized as a deadly drug and American children must be protected against it."

The lone voice against marijuana prohibition was Dr. William C. Woodward, a doctor and Chief Counsel to the American Medical Association (AMA), who testified that the AMA knew of no evidence that marijuana was dangerous. Woodward questioned the propriety of passing legislation based on personal opinion and asked why no data from the Bureau of Prisons or the Children's Bureau supported Anslinger's position. He also argued that the legislation would severely compromise a physician's ability to utilize marijuana's therapeutic potential. The committee showed no interest in Woodward's testimony, however, remarking, "If you want to advise us on legislation, you ought to come here with some constructive proposals . . . rather than trying to throw obstacles in the way of something that the federal government is trying to do." After only two hours of testimony before the committee, less than two minutes of testimony before Congress, and no debate at all before the Senate, the Marijuana Tax Act passed.

Anslinger had convinced Congress that marijuana was a dangerous, addictive drug. However, this position led to some unwanted results. Because of Anslinger's claim that marijuana caused mental illness, some lawyers successfully argued that the use of marijuana and the resulting insanity meant that some criminals should not be held accountable for their offenses. Still, the use of the insanity plea in these cases strengthened marijuana's reputation as a dangerous drug.

Congress, however, was not satisfied that the penalties were harsh enough to discourage the use of marijuana. Studies indicated that there had been a 77 percent increase for narcotics violations between 1948 and 1950. Moreover, movies like *High School Confidential* created the perception that high school students were starting to use drugs. So in 1951, Congress passed the Boggs Act, which nearly quadrupled the penalties for narcotics offenses and lumped marijuana together with narcotic drugs.

Once again, Anslinger's voice drowned out opposition by the medical community. During the hearings on the Boggs Act, doctors questioned whether marijuana was the dangerous drug that Anslinger and his supporters made it out to be. Dr. Harris Isbell, Director of Research at the Public Health Service hospital in Lexington, Kentucky, stated that marijuana was not physically addictive. In other testimony before a committee chaired by Senator Estes Kefauver, he testified that "Marijuana smokers generally are mildly intoxicated, giggle, laugh, bother no one, and have a good time. They do not stagger or fall, and ordinarily will not attempt to harm anyone. . . . It has not been proved that smoking marijuana leads to crimes of violence or to crimes of a sexual nature. Smoking marijuana has no unpleasant after-effects, no dependence is developed on the drug, and the practice can easily be stopped at any time. In fact, it is probably easier to stop smoking marijuana cigarettes than tobacco cigarettes."

Rather than contradict the doctor's testimony, Anslinger agreed. However, he argued that marijuana was the first step on the road to heroin addiction. This "gateway" theory quickly gained support. Representative Boggs himself mentioned during House debate, "Our younger people usually start on the road which leads to drug addiction by smoking marijuana. They then graduate into narcotic drugs—cocaine, morphine, and heroin. When these younger persons become addicted to the drugs, heroin, for example, which costs from $8 to $15 per day, they very often must embark on careers of crime . . . and prostitution . . . in order to buy the supply which they need." Anslinger's gateway theory convinced Congress to approve the Boggs Act.

The government's efforts to stop the spread of drug use seemed to be working, but out of concern that drugs were providing a source of income to organized crime, the enforcement focus shifted from those who bought drugs to those who sold them. As part of this shift, in 1956, Congress passed the Narcotic Control Act, also known as the Daniel Act, which increased the penalties for violation of the previous drug tax laws.

The new law raised the fine for all narcotics and marijuana offenses and increased the mandatory minimum sentences, making suspended sentences, probation, and parole for offenders unavailable. However, the heaviest penalties were for sale of drugs, especially to minors. The states passed similar acts, some with mandatory minimum sentences as long as forty years for the sale of marijuana.

The government's punitive approach to drugs soon came under fire. Reform-minded lawyers, academics, and physicians argued that addicts should not be jailed but hospitalized, believing that addiction should be treated as a disease instead of a crime. Some believed that Methadone, a synthetic opiate developed in Germany during World War II, was a possible solution to the problem of heroin addiction. Others believed that rehabilitation was the answer, and in 1966, civil commitment for addiction became possible.

By the late 1960s, public attitudes toward drugs had once again shifted. Research had shown that marijuana was less harmful than previously claimed. If the dangers of this drug had been overstated, the argument ran, perhaps it was time to reexamine laws against this and other drugs. Consequently, Congress passed the Controlled Substances Act, under which the penalties for drug use were lowered. The Act also abandoned the idea of using tax laws to control drug use. Although it was still illegal to possess addictive drugs other than nicotine and alcohol, the harsher penalties were reserved for those who sold drugs—particularly when the sale was to a minor. The same law also classified all drugs—even antibiotics—according to their potential for abuse and their significance as medicines.

Despite all the efforts by the government to discourage drug use, by 1971, it was clear that the laws were not working as planned. An evaluation of the government's drug policy by the National Commission on Marijuana and Drug Abuse found that rates of addiction had not dropped significantly. As part of its findings, the commission recommended decriminalization of marijuana to relieve law enforcement agencies of the burden of arresting individual users and to allow authorities to concentrate on investigating large-scale crime and more dangerous drugs. The recommendation was controversial, and then-President Richard Nixon refused to officially receive the report. Instead, Nixon declared that drugs were America's number one public enemy.

The president's declaration helped lend urgency to the debate over the government's drug policies. Moreover, in 1973, a second report made by the National Commission on Marijuana and Drug Abuse focused on the measurable damage of drug use and addiction. The report found, for example, that heroin—perceived to be one of the most deadly drugs—actually resulted in fewer deaths than barbiturates. In response, the federal government dedicated more funds to support anti-drug efforts and created the National Institute on Drug Abuse in 1974.

The federal policy toward drugs continued to evolve in the 1980s, in some ways returning to a focus on individual drug users. President Ronald Reagan's drug policy began with First Lady Nancy Reagan's "Just Say No" campaign. Rather than concerning itself with the forces that encouraged drug use and with those who sell drugs, the campaign emphasized the individual's responsibility for avoiding drug use. Holding individuals accountable took another step forward in 1988, with the passage of a law that imposed civil penalties of as much as $10,000 for possession of even small quantities of illegal drugs.

By the late 1980s, some in the government were ready to declare victory in the war on drugs. In 1989, for example, former President Ronald Reagan claimed that casual drug use had diminished by 37 percent between 1979 and 1989. However, twenty to forty million people still used drugs, and when President George Bush addressed the nation on September 5, 1989, he outlined his strategy for eradicating drug use, calling on Congress to spend $7.2 billion for his war on drugs. Congress granted this request. Of this funding, 70 percent went to law enforcement, including $1.6 billion for jails. Only 30 percent went to prevention, education, and treatment. The Bush administration waged its war by focusing on an enforcement approach—arresting, rather than rehabilitating the drug user.

As the twentieth century closed, the government's response to drugs continued to be a matter of debate. Many who had once supported prohibition of drugs and who had been staunch supporters of the war on drugs began to question the efficacy of United States policy toward drugs and drug abuse. Even the conservative author and journalist William F. Buckley Jr., who had previously supported the government's drug policy, came to argue that the costs of prohibition were too high, hurting not only users, but nonusers whose lives are put at risk by the criminal practices of users. However, Buckley noted that his was not a popular position, saying "most Americans think that voting in favor of legalization is like voting in favor of drugs." As a consequence, U.S. drug policy continued to oppose drug legalization.

The debate over legalization has continued into the twenty-first century. Some continue to support strong legislative measures to combat drug use, arguing that the government must protect its citizens from the dangers of drug abuse. These opponents claim that legalization of any kind would not only increase drug use but other crime as well. Others argue that decriminalization and regulation of drug sales represent more humane solutions, claiming that not only is America losing the war on drugs but the casualties of the war far outweigh any intended benefits. Still others argue for outright legalization, reasoning that the U.S. Constitution prohibits government interference in the personal choice to use or abuse drugs. Whether arguing for decriminalization, regulation, legalization, or continued prohibition of drugs, the authors of the viewpoints in this volume continue the drug policy debate.

1

The Legalization of Drugs Requires Serious Scrutiny

Paul B. Stares

Paul B. Stares is a senior fellow in Foreign Policy Studies at the Brookings Institute, a public policy think tank in Washington, D.C., where his expertise includes drug policy. Stares is also the author of Global Habit: The Drug Problem in a Borderless World.

Whenever people discuss the drug problem in the United States, some argue for tougher laws and stiffer penalties while others claim that because the government is losing the war on drugs and prohibition encourages crime, drugs should be legalized. However, an actual study of the regulatory alternatives is necessary to evaluate whether legalization would be an effective policy. The government must study what drugs would be legalized and in what form they would be available; who would produce the legal drugs and how would the producer be regulated; for whom would drugs be available, in what quantity, and under what conditions? Only when the government studies all alternatives can the actual costs and benefits of legalization be evaluated.

Whether Bill Clinton "inhaled" when trying marijuana as a college student was about the closest the 1992 presidential campaign came to addressing the drug issue. The 1996 campaign, however, could be very different. For the fourth straight year, a federally supported nationwide survey of American secondary school students by the University of Michigan has indicated increased drug use. After a decade or more in which drug use had been falling, the Republicans will assuredly blame the bad news on President Clinton and assail him for failing to carry on the Bush and Reagan administrations' high-profile stand against drugs. How big this issue becomes is less certain, but if the worrisome trend in drug use among teens continues, public debate about how best to respond to the drug problem will clearly not end with the election. Indeed, concern is already mounting that the large wave of teenagers—the group most at risk of taking drugs—that will crest around

Reprinted from Paul B. Stares, "Drug Legalization: Time for a Real Debate," *The Brookings Review*, Spring 1996. Reprinted with permission from Cynthia Strauss-Ortiz at the Brookings Institute Press.

the turn of the century will be accompanied by a new surge in drug use.

As in the past, some observers will doubtless see the solution in much tougher penalties to deter both suppliers and consumers of illicit psychoactive substances. Others will argue that the answer lies not in more law enforcement and stiffer sanctions, but in less. Specifically, they will maintain that the edifice of domestic laws and international conventions that collectively prohibit the production, sale, and consumption of a large array of drugs for anything other than medical or scientific purposes has proven physically harmful, socially divisive, prohibitively expensive, and ultimately counterproductive in generating the very incentives that perpetuate a violent black market for illicit drugs. They will conclude, moreover, that the only logical step for the United States to take is to "legalize" drugs—in essence repeal and disband the current drug laws and enforcement mechanisms in much the same way America abandoned its brief experiment with alcohol prohibition in the 1920s.

Each time the issue of legalization arises, the same arguments for and against are dusted off and trotted out, leaving us with no clearer understanding.

Although the legalization alternative typically surfaces when the public's anxiety about drugs and despair over existing policies are at their highest, it never seems to slip off the media radar screen for long. Periodic incidents—such as the heroin-induced death of a young, affluent New York City couple in 1995 or the 1993 remark by then Surgeon General Jocelyn Elders that legalization might be beneficial and should be studied—ensure this. The prominence of many of those who have at various times made the case for legalization—such as William F. Buckley, Jr., Milton Friedman, and George Shultz—also helps. But each time the issue of legalization arises, the same arguments for and against are dusted off and trotted out, leaving us with no clearer understanding of what it might entail and what the effect might be.

A need for serious debate

As will become clear, drug legalization is not a public policy option that lends itself to simplistic or superficial debate. It requires dissection and scrutiny of an order that has been remarkably absent despite the attention it perennially receives. Beyond discussion of some very generally defined proposals, there has been no detailed assessment of the operational meaning of legalization. There is not even a commonly accepted lexicon of terms to allow an intellectually rigorous exchange to take place. Legalization, as a consequence, has come to mean different things to different people. Some, for example, use legalization interchangeably with "decriminalization," which usually refers to removing criminal sanctions for possessing small quantities of drugs for personal use. Others equate legalization, at least implicitly, with complete deregulation, failing in the process to acknowledge the extent to which currently legally available drugs are subject to stringent controls.

Unfortunately, the U.S. government—including the Clinton administration—has done little to improve the debate. Although it has consistently rejected any retreat from prohibition, its stance has evidently not been based on in-depth investigation of the potential costs and benefits. The belief that legalization would lead to an instant and dramatic increase in drug use is considered to be so self-evident as to warrant no further study. But if this is indeed the likely conclusion of any study, what is there to fear aside from criticism that relatively small amounts of taxpayer money had been wasted in demonstrating what everyone had believed at the outset? Wouldn't such an outcome in any case help justify the continuation of existing policies and convincingly silence those—admittedly never more than a small minority—calling for legalization?

A real debate that acknowledges the unavoidable complexities and uncertainties surrounding the notion of drug legalization is long overdue. Not only would it dissuade people from making the kinds of casual if not flippant assertions—both for and against—that have permeated previous debates about legalization, but it could also stimulate a larger and equally critical assessment of current U.S. drug control programs and priorities.

Many arguments appear to make legalization a compelling alternative to today's prohibitionist policies. Besides undermining the black-market incentives to produce and sell drugs, legalization could remove or at least significantly reduce the very problems that cause the greatest public concern: the crime, corruption, and violence that attend the operation of illicit drug markets. It would presumably also diminish the damage caused by the absence of quality controls on illicit drugs and slow the spread of infectious diseases due to needle sharing and other unhygienic practices. Furthermore, governments could abandon the costly and largely futile effort to suppress the supply of illicit drugs and jail drug offenders, spending the money thus saved to educate people not to take drugs and treat those who become addicted.

Until all the principal alternatives are clearly laid out in reasonable detail, however, the potential costs and benefits of each cannot begin to be responsibly assessed.

However, what is typically portrayed as a fairly straightforward process of lifting prohibitionist controls to reap these putative benefits would in reality entail addressing an extremely complex set of regulatory issues. As with most if not all privately and publicly provided goods, the key regulatory questions concern the nature of the legally available drugs, the terms of their supply, and the terms of their consumption.

Examining all the alternatives

What becomes immediately apparent from even a casual review of these questions—and the list presented here is by no means exhaustive—is that there is an enormous range of regulatory permutations for each drug. Until all the principal alternatives are clearly laid out in reasonable detail, however, the potential costs and benefits of each cannot begin to be responsibly assessed. This fundamental point can be illustrated with respect to the two central questions most likely to sway public opinion. What would happen to drug consumption under more permissive regulatory regimes? And what would happen to crime?

> *Jettisoning nearly a century of prohibition when the putative benefits remain so uncertain and the potential costs are so high would require a herculean leap of faith.*

Relaxing the availability of psychoactive substances not already commercially available, opponents typically argue, would lead to an immediate and substantial rise in consumption. To support their claim, they point to the prevalence of opium, heroin, and cocaine addiction in various countries before international controls took effect, the rise in alcohol consumption after the Volstead Act was repealed in the United States, and studies showing higher rates of abuse among medical professionals with greater access to prescription drugs. Without explaining the basis of their calculations, some have predicted dramatic increases in the number of people taking drugs and becoming addicted. These increases would translate into considerable direct and indirect costs to society, including higher public health spending as a result of drug overdoses, fetal deformities, and other drug-related misadventures such as auto accidents; loss of productivity due to worker absenteeism and on-the-job accidents; and more drug-induced violence, child abuse, and other crimes, to say nothing about educational impairment.

Advocates of legalization concede that consumption would probably rise, but counter that it is not axiomatic that the increase would be very large or last very long, especially if legalization were paired with appropriate public education programs. They too cite historical evidence to bolster their claims, noting that consumption of opium, heroin, and cocaine had already begun falling before prohibition took effect, that alcohol consumption did not rise suddenly after prohibition was lifted, and that decriminalization of cannabis use in 11 U.S. states in the 1970s did not precipitate a dramatic rise in its consumption. Some also point to the legal sale of cannabis products through regulated outlets in the Netherlands, which also does not seem to have significantly boosted use by Dutch nationals. Public opinion polls showing that most Americans would not rush off to try hitherto forbidden drugs that suddenly became available are likewise used to buttress the pro-legalization case.

Neither side's arguments are particularly reassuring. The historical evidence is ambiguous at best, even assuming that the experience of one era is relevant to another. Extrapolating the results of policy steps in one country to another with different sociocultural values runs into the same problem. Similarly, within the United States the effect of decriminalization at the state level must be viewed within the general context of continued federal prohibition. And opinion polls are known to be unreliable.

More to the point, until the nature of the putative regulatory regime is specified, such discussions are futile. It would be surprising, for example, if consumption of the legalized drugs did not increase if they were to become commercially available the way that alcohol and tobacco products are today, complete with sophisticated packaging, marketing, and advertising. But more restrictive regimes might see quite different outcomes. In any case, the risk of higher drug consumption might be acceptable if legalization could reduce dramatically if not remove entirely the crime associated with the black market for illicit drugs while also making some forms of drug use safer. Here again, there are disputed claims.

Opponents of more permissive regimes doubt that black market activity and its associated problems would disappear or even fall very much. But, as before, addressing this question requires knowing the specifics of the regulatory regime, especially the terms of supply. If drugs are sold openly on a commercial basis and prices are close to production and distribution costs, opportunities for illicit undercutting would appear to be rather small. Under a more restrictive regime, such as government-controlled outlets or medical prescription schemes, illicit sources of supply would be more likely to remain or evolve to satisfy the legally unfulfilled demand. In short, the desire to control access to stem consumption has to be balanced against the black market opportunities that would arise. Schemes that risk a continuing black market require more questions—about the new black markets operation over time, whether it is likely to be more benign than existing ones, and more broadly whether the trade-off with other benefits still makes the effort worthwhile.

The most obvious case is regulating access to drugs by adolescents and young adults. Under any regime, it is hard to imagine that drugs that are now prohibited would become more readily available than alcohol and tobacco are today. Would a black market in drugs for teenagers emerge, or would the regulatory regime be as leaky as the present one for alcohol and tobacco? A "yes" answer to either question would lessen the attractiveness of legalization.

The international repercussions?

Not surprisingly, the wider international ramifications of drug legalization have also gone largely unremarked. Here too a long set of questions remains to be addressed. Given the longstanding U.S. role as the principal sponsor of international drug control measures, how would a decision to move toward legalizing drugs affect other countries? What would become of the extensive regime of multilateral conventions and bilateral agreements? Would every nation have to conform to a new set of rules? If not, what would happen? Would more permissive countries be suddenly swamped by drugs and drug consumers, or would traffickers focus on the countries where tighter restrictions kept profits higher? This is not an abstract question. The Netherlands' liberal drug policy has attracted an influx of "drug tourists" from neighboring countries, as did the city of Zurich's following the now abandoned experiment allowing an open drug market to operate in what became known as "Needle Park." And while it is conceivable that affluent countries could soften the worst consequences of drug legalization through extensive public prevention and drug treatment programs, what about poorer countries?

Finally, what would happen to the principal suppliers of illicit drugs if restrictions on the commercial sale of these drugs were lifted in some or all of the main markets? Would the trafficking organizations adapt and become legal businesses or turn to other illicit enterprises? What would happen to the source countries? Would they benefit or would new producers and manufacturers suddenly spring up elsewhere? Such questions have not even been posed in a systematic way, let alone seriously studied.

The uncertainties of permissive regulation

Although greater precision in defining more permissive regulatory regimes is critical to evaluating their potential costs and benefits, it will not resolve the uncertainties that exist. Only implementation will do that. Because small-scale experimentation (assuming a particular locality's consent to be a guinea pig) would inevitably invite complaints that the results were biased or inconclusive, implementation would presumably have to be widespread, even global, in nature.

Yet jettisoning nearly a century of prohibition when the putative benefits remain so uncertain and the potential costs are so high would require a herculean leap of faith. Only an extremely severe and widespread deterioration of the current drug situation, nationally and internationally—is likely to produce the consensus—again, nationally and internationally that could impel such a leap. Even then the legislative challenge would be stupendous. The debate over how to set the conditions for controlling access to each of a dozen popular drugs could consume the legislatures of the major industrial countries for years.

None of this should deter further analysis of drug legalization. In particular, a rigorous assessment of a range of hypothetical regulatory regimes according to a common set of variables would clarify their potential costs, benefits, and trade-offs. Besides instilling much-needed rigor into any further discussion of the legalization alternative, such analysis could encourage the same level of scrutiny of current drug control programs and policies. With the situation apparently deteriorating in the United States as well as abroad, there is no better time for a fundamental reassessment of whether our existing responses to this problem are sufficient to meet the likely challenges ahead.

2

Prohibiting Drugs Has Serious Consequences

Joshua Wolf Shenk

Joshua Wolf Shenk is a freelance writer living in New York City who has written many articles on legalization and drug policy for magazines such as Harper's, *the* Washington Monthly, *and* The Economist.

Although the horrors of drug addiction appear to call for prohibition, the war on drugs has created its own victims: innocent children killed in drug-related shootouts, young people lured from school into the drug trade, and nonviolent criminals imprisoned for unreasonably long terms. Instead of spending tax dollars building more prisons and fighting a losing battle, the government should spend money on treatment and education. Drugs are indeed dangerous, yet the government chooses to regulate, not prohibit equally dangerous drugs like tobacco and alcohol. Rather than continue its crusade against drugs, the government should examine alternatives to prohibition.

There's no breeze, only bare, stifling heat, but Kevin can scarcely support his wispy frame. He bobs forward, his eyes slowly closing until he drifts asleep, in a 45-degree hunch. "Kevin?" I say softly. He jerks awake and slowly rubs a hand over his spindly chest. "It's so hot in here I can hardly think," he says.

Kevin is wearing an "Americorps" baseball cap, and I ask him where he got it. The lids close over his glassy eyes and then open again, showing a look of gentle, but deep confusion. He removes the hat, revealing hair the tone of a red shirt that's been through the washer a thousand times. He blinks again and glances at the cap. He has no idea.

In July 1995, I spent a long, hot day talking to junkies in New York City, in a run-down hotel near Columbia University. Some, like Kevin, were reticent. Others spoke freely about their lives and addictions. I sat with Melissa for 20 minutes as she patiently hunted her needle-scarred legs for a vein to take a spike. She had just fixed after a long dry spell. "I was sick," she told me. "I could hardly move. And Papo"—she gestures toward a friend sitting across from her—"he helped me out. He gave me something to make me better."

To most Americans, addicts like Kevin and Melissa and Papo are not people, but arguments. Some victims of drug use inspire sympathy, or irritation, or just plain worry. But it is the junkies—seemingly bereft of humanity, subsisting in what one former addict calls "soul-death"—who justify our national attitude toward certain drugs: that they should be illegal, unavailable, and totally suppressed.

The victims of the drug trade

But this country has another drug problem, one with its own tragic stories. In 1993, Launice Smith was killed in a shoot-out between rival drug dealers at a football game at an elementary school in Washington, D.C. There were four other murder victims in the same neighborhood that day. Launice stood out, though, because she was only four years old.

Addicts suffer from illegal drugs. But each year hundreds of children like Launice are killed *because* drugs are illegal. It's difficult, but crucial, to understand this distinction. By turning popular drugs into illegal contraband, prohibition sparks tremendous inflation. Small amounts of plant leaves and powder that cost only pennies to grow and process sell for hundreds of dollars on the street. All told, the black market in this country takes in $50 to $60 billion in income each year. In lawful society, such a large industry would be regulated by rules and enforcement mechanisms. But the intense competition of the black market is regulated only by violence. Rival entrepreneurs don't go to the courts with a dispute. They shoot it out in the street.

The black market now holds entire communities in its grip. In addition to the violence—and crime driven by addicts supporting expensive habits—the fast cash of dealing lures many young people away from school, into the drug trade, and often onto a track toward jail or death.

Government does have a responsibility to limit the individual and social costs of drug use, but such efforts must be balanced against the harm they cause.

We are caught, then, between the Kevins and the Launices, between the horror of drug abuse and the horror of the illegal drug trade. Making drugs legally available, with tight regulatory controls, would end the black market, and with it much of the violence, crime, and social pathology we have come to understand as "drug-related." And yet, history shows clearly that lifting prohibition would allow for more drug use, and more abuse and addiction.

I spent that day in New York to face this excruciating dilemma. It's easy to call for an end to prohibition from an office in Washington, D.C. What about when looking into Kevin's dim eyes, or confronting the images of crack babies, shriveled and wincing?

The choice between two intensely unpleasant options is never easy. But, considering this problem in all its depth and complexity, it becomes clear that drug prohibition does more harm than good. We can't discount the problem of drug abuse (and that includes the abuse of legal drugs). But prohibition didn't keep Kevin from becoming an addict in the first place, and it certainly isn't helping him stop. High prices for drugs do discourage some would-be users, though far fewer than the government would like. The fact is we have done a very poor job discouraging drug use with the blunt force of law. The hundreds of billions of dollars spent on drug control in the last several decades have yielded only a moderate decline in the casual use of marijuana and cocaine. But there has been no decrease in hard-core addiction. The total amount of cocaine consumed per capita has actually risen. And even casual use is creeping up.

In communities where two-thirds of the youth lack the schooling or skills to get a decent job, drug dealing is both lucrative and glamorous.

Government does have a responsibility to limit the individual and social costs of drug use, but such efforts must be balanced against the harm they cause. And ending the drug war needn't mean a surrender to addiction, or an affirmation of reckless drug use. President Bill Clinton's stance on cigarette addiction—that cigarettes can be both legal and tightly regulated, particularly with respect to advertising aimed at children—points to a middle ground. Potentially, we could do a better job of fighting drug abuse, while avoiding the vicious side-effects of an outright ban.

Comparing the costs

Unfortunately, this country's discussion of "the drug problem" is marked by little clear analysis and much misinformation. Politicians and bureaucrats minimize or entirely ignore the consequences of prohibition. At the other extreme, libertarians call for government to withdraw from regulating intoxicants entirely. The press, meanwhile, does little to illuminate the costs and benefits of the current prohibition or our many other policy options. "We don't cover drug policy, except episodically as a cops and robbers story," says Max Frankel, the recently retired executive editor of *The New York Times*. He calls his paper's coverage of the subject "one of my failures there as an editor, and a failure of newspapers generally."

It's not that the consequences of prohibition can't be seen in the newspapers. In the *Times* last December 1994, for example, Isabel Wilkerson wrote a stirring profile of Jovan Rogers, a Chicago crack dealer who entered the trade when he was 14 and ended up crippled by gunshot wounds. But Wilkerson, as reporters usually do, conveyed the impression that the pathology of the black market is unfortunate, but inevitable—not the result of policies that we can change.

In fact, Rogers' story is a vivid display of the lethal drug trade that prohibition creates, the temptation of bright young men, and the cycle of destruction that soon follows.

For his first job, Rogers got $75 a day to watch out for the police. Soon, he was earning thousands a day. And though Rogers said he began dealing to support his family—"If there's nothing to eat at night," he asked, "who's going to go buy something to make sure something is there? I was the only man in the house"—the big bucks also seized him where, like most teenagers, he was most vulnerable. "If you sell drugs, you had anything you wanted," he said. "Any girl, any friend, money, status. If you didn't, you got no girlfriend, no friends, no money. You're a nothing."

This story is all too common. In communities where two-thirds of the youth lack the schooling or skills to get a decent job, drug dealing is both lucrative and glamorous. Rich dealers are role models and images of entrepreneurial success—the Bill Gateses of the inner city. Unlike straight jobs, though, dealing drugs means entering a world of gruesome violence. Like all initiates, Rogers was issued a gun, and learned quickly to shoot—to discipline other dealers in the gang or to battle rival gangs for control over a corner or neighborhood. Sometimes he would shoot blindly, out of raw fear. Newspapers report stories of "drug-related" murder. But drug *war* murder is more like it. The illegal drug trade is the country's leading cause of death by homicide—and the illegal drug trade wouldn't exist without prohibition.

Although it is popular these days to blame welfare for undermining the work ethic, often overlooked is the role played by the black market's twisted incentives, which lure men away from school and legitimate work—and, often, away from their families. In a recent two-page spread, *The Washington Post* celebrated successful students at the city's Eastern High School. Of the 76 students pictured, 64 were women—only 12 were men. The school's principal, Ralph Neal, acknowledges the role of the drug trade with a sigh, calling it a "tremendous temptation."

Writ large, the black market eventually consumes entire neighborhoods. At one time, the area of Philadelphia now referred to as "Badlands" was peppered with factories, mom-and-pop grocery stores, taverns, and theaters. Now drug dealers are positioned on street corners and in flashy cars, poised to fire their guns at the slightest provocation. Crack vials and dirty needles line the streets. Often, customers drive through in BMWs with New Jersey plates, making their buys and then scurrying back to the suburbs.

The system is overloaded with non-violent drug users and dealers, who now often receive harsher penalties than murderers, rapists, and serious white collar criminals.

Of course, impoverished communities like this one have more troubles than just drug prohibition. But it is the black market, residents will tell you, that is a noose around their neck. Drive-by shootings and deadly stray bullets are bad enough, but some of the most devastating casualties are indirect ones. This summer two children suffocated while playing in an abandoned car in Southeast Washington. The kids avoided local playgrounds, one child said, because they feared "bullies and drug dealers."

"Kids in the inner city are scared to go to school," says Philippe Bourgois, a scholar who spent three and a half years with drug dealers in East

Harlem writing *In Search of Respect: Selling Crack in El Barrio.* "You're going to pass five or six dealers hawking vials of crack on your way there. You face getting mugged in the hallway. The dealers . . . they drop out, but they don't stop going to school—that's where the action is."

Drug prohibition is very much of a crusade, discussed in moral terms, supported on faith, not evidence.

A D.C. public school teacher told me that 13-year-old dealers, already fully initiated into the drug culture, crawl through a hole in the fence around her school's playground to talk to fifth and sixth graders. Once, after she and a security guard chased them off, a group of young dealers found her in the school's parking lot. "There's that snitching bitch," one kid said. "That's the bitch that snitched. I'm going to kill you, you snitching bitch." The drug war's Dr. Seuss.

A nation behind bars

The high prices caused by prohibition drive crime in another way: Addicts need cash to feed their habits. The junkies I met in New York told me they would spend between $200 and $600 a week for drugs. Melissa, for example, once had a good job and made enough to pay her bills and to buy dope. Then she got laid off and turned to prostitution to support her habit. Others steal to pay for their drugs—from liquor stores, from their families, from dealers, or from other addicts. According to a study by the Bureau of Justice Statistics, one out of every three thefts are committed by people seeking drug money.

This crime wave does not restrict itself to the inner cities. Addicts seeking money to get a fix are very fond of the fine appliances and cash-filled wallets found in wealthier neighborhoods. Suburban high schools may not have swarms of dealers crawling through the fences, but dealers are there too. In fact, the suburbs are increasingly popular for dealers looking to take up residence.

Quite apart from the costs of the black market—the crime, the neighborhoods and lives ruined—Americans also pay a heavy price for the drug war itself. For fiscal 1996, Clinton has requested $14.6 billion for drug control (up from only $1.3 billion in 1983). State and local governments spend about twice that each year.

But these budgets reflect only a small portion of the costs. In 1980, the United States had 330,000 people in jail; today, it's well over a million, and drug offenders account for 46 percent of that increase. On top of the cost of building prisons, it takes more than $30,000 per year to keep someone in jail. Naturally, prison spending has exploded. The country now spends nearly $30 billion annually on corrections. Between 1970 and 1990, state and local governments hiked prison spending by 232 percent.

Even worse, thanks to mandatory minimum sentences, the system is overloaded with non-violent drug users and dealers, who now often receive harsher penalties than murderers, rapists, and serious white collar criminals. Solicited by an undercover DEA agent to find a cocaine supplier, Gary Fannon facilitated the deal and received a sentence of life without parole. Larry Singleton raped a teenager, hacked off her arms between the wrist and elbow, and left her for dead in the desert. He received the 14-year maximum sentence and served only eight years. This disparity is not the exception in modern law enforcement. It is the rule. Nonviolent drug offenders receive an average 60 months in jail time, *five times* the average 12-month-sentence for manslaughter convicts.

Some people may say: Build more jails. In an era of tax cuts and fiscal freezes, though, every dollar spent on corrections comes from roads, or health care, or education. Even with the huge growth in prison spending, three-fourths of all state prisons were operating over their maximum capacity in 1992. Even conservatives like Michael Quinlan, director of the federal Bureau of Prisons under Reagan and Bush, have had enough of this insanity. "They're locking up a lot of people who are not serious or violent offenders," he says. "That . . . brings serious consequences in terms of our ability to incarcerate truly violent criminals."

What we have had a hard time learning is that there are a plethora of options between prohibition and laissez-faire.

If sticking a drug dealer in jail meant fewer dealers on the street, perhaps this wave of incarceration would eventually do some good. But it doesn't work like that: Lock up a murderer, and you have one less murderer on the street. Lock up a dealer, and you create a job opening. It's like jailing an IBM executive; the pay is good, the job is appealing, so someone will move into the office before long. Clearing dealers from one neighborhood only means they'll move to another. Busting a drug ring only makes room for a competitor. "We put millions of drug offenders through the courts—and we have more people in jail per capita than any country except Russia—but we're not affecting the drug trade, let alone drug use," says Robert Sweet, U.S. district judge in the Southern district of New York.

"It's perfectly obvious," Sweet says, "that if you took the money spent housing drug offenders and enforcing the drug laws, and apply it to straight law enforcement, the results would be very impressive." Indeed, what politicians ignore is all too clear to judges, prosecutors, and cops. "The drug war can't be won," says Joseph McNamara, the former chief of police in Kansas City and San Jose, who also spent 10 years on the New York City force. "Any cop will tell you that."

What makes it even tougher for law enforcement is the pervasiveness of corruption spawned by the black market in drugs. In May 1992, New York City police uncovered the largest corruption scandal in the department's 146-year history, most of it, according to the commission that investigated it, involving "groups of officers . . . identifying drug sites; planning raids; forcibly entering and looting drug trafficking locations, and sharing proceeds." There have been similar stories recently in Philadelphia, Washington, D.C., New Orleans, and Atlanta. Sadly, in movies like *The Bad Lieutenant*, art is imitating life. Cops shake down dealers, steal their cash, and sometimes deal the drugs themselves. Or they take bribes to protect dealers from arrest.

Despite these drug war casualties—and the dismal progress in stemming drug use—each year the war intensifies. Politicians from Newt Gingrich to Bill Bradley now push for expanding the death penalty for dealers. But experience shows that the deterrent effect will be negligible. "There is no evidence that increasing penalties for drug dealing deters people from doing it," says Quinlan. "It just doesn't work like that—not when your chances of getting caught are so low, and the profits are so high." As Quinlan points out, the DEA and White House count it as a success if drug prices are driven up, but that only makes the problem worse. On the streets, meanwhile, we have the worst of both worlds: Drugs are expensive enough to fuel a deadly black market, but people still buy them.

Illegal drugs, left unregulated, are also much more dangerous than they need to be. Imagine drinking whisky with no idea of its potency. It could be 30 proof or 190 proof—or diluted with a dangerous chemical. One addict I met, Mary, had blood-red sores running up her arms—from cocaine cut with meat tenderizer. Virtually all "overdose" deaths from the use of illegal drugs are due to contaminants or the user's ignorance of the drug's potency. "Just desserts," one might say. But isn't the basis of our drug policy supposed to be concern for people's health and well-being?

Unfortunately, this country's leaders have lost sight of that principle. "Policies," Thomas Sowell has written, "are judged by their consequences, but crusades are judged by how good they make the crusaders feel." Drug prohibition is very much of a crusade, discussed in moral terms, supported on faith, not evidence. The DEA stages high-profile drug raids—covered dutifully in newspapers and magazines—but is never able to limit supply. The government sends troops to burn poppy in South America and stubbornly insists, despite overwhelming evidence to the contrary, that interdiction can make a real difference in keeping drugs out of the country.

Meanwhile, drug treatment—no panacea, but certainly more effective in limiting drug use than law enforcement or interdiction—is continually underfunded. Candidate Clinton promised "treatment on demand" in 1992, but President Clinton has not delivered. Like Reagan and Bush, he has spent about two-thirds of the anti-drug budget on law enforcement and interdiction.

Beyond government, we must recognize as a culture the damage done by drugs—even if we accept the rights of individuals to use them.

For a real blood boiler, consider the case of pregnant women addicted to drugs. Lee Brown, White House director of drug policy control, often talks of visiting crack babies in the hospital to shame those who would liberalize drug laws. But, like many addicts, pregnant women often avoid treatment or health care because they fear arrest.

Although it's hard to believe, those who do seek help—for themselves and their unborn children—are often turned away. David Condliffe, who was the director of drug policy for New York City in the late eighties, conducted a survey that found that 85 percent of poor, pregnant crack addicts looking for treatment were refused everywhere they tried. Nationwide, treatment is available for only 10 percent of the 300,000 pregnant women who abuse illegal drugs. This is perhaps the greatest moral horror of our current policy—and it should shame everyone from President Clinton on down.

Beyond the crusade

Regardless of your stance on drug policy, there can be no disagreement that we must demand honesty from public officials on this subject. Forget for a moment reporters' nonfeasance in covering the nuances of drug policy. When it comes to the drug war, they're also failing to expose coverups and outright lies.

As just one example, consider the case of needle exchange. Forty percent of new AIDS cases reported in 1992 (24,000 in total) came from infection through use of dirty needles. But the federal government continues to ban the use of AIDS-prevention funds for programs that replace dirty needles with clean ones.

This despite the fact that in 1994 the Centers for Disease Control issued a report concluding that needle exchange *does not* encourage heroin use, but *does* dramatically reduce HIV transmission. The report explicitly recommends that the federal ban be lifted. The Clinton Administration suppressed the report, but a copy finally leaked. Now, officials deny its basic finding. "(The CDC) pointed out that the jury is still out on needle exchange," Lee Brown told me. Either he hasn't read the report, or he is lying.

Even more infuriating, supporters of the drug war insist on confusing the harms of drug use with the harms of prohibition. William Bennett, for example, cites "murder and mayhem being committed on our cities' streets" as justification to intensify the drug war, when, as Milton Friedman wrote in an open letter to Bennett, "the very measures you favor are a major source of the evils you deplore." Meanwhile, in the current political climate, the likes of Joycelyn Elders—who merely suggested we *study* the link between prohibition and violence—are shouted down.

Facing drug abuse

Cocaine can cause heart attacks in people prone to irregular heartbeats, such as basketball star Len Bias, and seizures in people with mild epilepsy; it's even more dangerous mixed with alcohol and other drugs. Heroin can lead to intense physical dependence—withdrawal symptoms include nausea, convulsions, and loss of bowel control. Even marijuana can be psychologically addictive; smoking too much dope can lead to respiratory problems or even cancer.

Illegal drugs have social costs as well. Consistent intoxication—whether it's a gram-a-day coke fiend, or a regular pot smoker with a miserable memory—can mean lost productivity, increased accidents, and fractured relationships.

And addiction . . . well, it's not pretty. Coke addicts often suffer acute depression without a fix. Heroin is even worse. David Morrison, recalling his furious struggle with heroin addiction in *Washington City Paper*, describes the misery of waiting for his dealer: "If sweet oblivion is the initial carrot, savage withdrawal is the enduring stick. In time, the dope fiend is not so much chasing a high as fleeing a debacle."

Given the terrible consequences of drug abuse, any reasonable person is bound to object: How could we even consider making drugs generally available? But have you asked why alcohol and tobacco are kept generally available?

Tobacco products—linked to cancer of the lungs, throat, larynx, and ovaries—cause 30 percent of all cancer deaths. Even more tobacco-related deaths come from heart attacks and strokes. Every year 435,000 Americans die premature deaths because of cigarettes. And, of course, nicotine is extremely addictive: The Surgeon General has found that the "capture" rate—the percentage of people who become addicted after trying it—is higher with cigarettes than any other drug, legal or illegal. Most nicotine addicts are hooked before age 18.

Alcohol is even more destructive. Extensive drinking often results in bleeding ulcers, cirrhosis of the liver, stomach and intestinal inflammation, and muscle damage as well as severe damage to the brain and nervous system, manifested by blackouts and psychotic episodes.

As for social costs, alcohol is the most likely of all mind-altering substances to induce criminal behavior, according to the National Institute of Justice. Close to 11 million Americans are alcoholics, and another 7 million are alcohol abusers—meaning they've screwed up at work, been in an accident, or been arrested because of drinking. Drunk driving is the cause of a third of all traffic fatalities. Alcohol-related problems affect one out of every four American homes, and alcoholism is involved in 60 percent of all murders and 38 percent of child abuse cases. These statistics only confirm our everyday experience. Who doesn't know of a family shattered by an alcoholic, or someone who has suffered with an alcoholic boss?

The reason that alcohol and tobacco are legal, despite the damage they do, is that prohibition would be even worse. In the case of alcohol, we know from experience. The prohibition from 1919 to 1933 is now synonymous with violence, organized crime, and corruption. Financed by huge profits from bootlegging, gangsters like Al Capone terrorized cities and eluded the best efforts of law enforcement. It soon became too much.

After prohibition's repeal, consumption rates for alcohol did in fact rise. But as anyone who was alive in 1933 could tell you, the increase was hardly an explosion. And it seems likely that the rise was fueled by advertising and the movies. Drunks were likeable (bit-player Jack Norton played the amiable falling-down drunk in scores of movies of that era) or even glamorous (like William Powell in *The Thin Man* films). It took years for government, the media, and entertainers to realize their responsibility to push temperance—and even now they're not doing all they can.

Finding other options

What we have had a hard time learning is that there are a plethora of options between prohibition and laissez-faire. In 1933, after prohibition, the federal government withdrew entirely from regulating the market in spirits. No limits were placed on marketing or advertising, and the siege from Madison Avenue and Hollywood began immediately. For years, the government seemed unable to counter the excesses of legal drug pushers like Philip Morris and Seagrams. Ads for tobacco, beer and liquor dominated the worlds of art and entertainment.

The tide began to turn in 1964, when the Surgeon General issued the first of a series of reports on the dangers of smoking. In 1971 cigarette ads were banned from TV and radio. The media began to open its eyes as well. Meanwhile, there was an equally important change in attitudes. It was once respectable to drink two or three martinis at a business lunch. Today it is not. Nor do we wink at drunk driving or smoking by pregnant women. Cigarette use, in fact, has declined dramatically since the sixties.

But much has been left undone. The TV and radio ban, for example, left the bulk of cigarette marketing untouched. And ironically, tobacco companies didn't much mind the ban, because it also dealt a severe blow to a campaign of negative advertising. Under the "fairness doctrine," TV and radio stations in the late sixties gave free air time to anti-smoking spots, such as one that mocked the Marlboro man by showing him coughing and wheezing. These ads were extremely effective, more so, many believed, than the Surgeon General's warnings. Once the tobacco ads were banned, though, TV and radio stations were no longer required to run the negative spots.

We will always have a "drug problem" of some sort. The question is: What kind of drug problem?

It is high time to begin a massive campaign of negative advertising against both cigarettes and alcohol. And we can ban advertising for intoxicants entirely. President Clinton, who has moved to restrict advertising that encourages smoking *and* to require tobacco companies to pay for a campaign against smoking, has taken a step in the right direction.

In a recent essay in *The New Republic*, Thomas Laqueur criticized Clinton's initiative on cigarette advertising as the product of "prohibitionist energies." But this is the simple-minded either/or attitude that got us into such a mess. Yes, cigarettes and alcohol ought to be legally available. But that doesn't mean we can't curb the pushers, educate people about the dangers, and generally try to reduce the harm.

The same approach should be employed with now-illegal drugs. An end to prohibition need not mean official endorsement of crack or heroin, but instead could be an opportunity to redouble efforts to limit their use. Drug use would rise after prohibition—but it wouldn't be the catastrophic explosion that drug warriors predict. They count on both distortions of history (claiming an explosion of alcohol use in 1933) and exaggerations of the dangers of cocaine, heroin, and speed—not to mention marijuana and hallucinogens. Though all intoxicants should be taken seriously, these drugs are neither as powerful, addictive, or attractive as many imagine. Among the population of non-users, 97 percent of Americans say they would be "not very likely" or "not at all likely" to try cocaine if it were legal. And even those who would try it in a legal regime would not find themselves immediately in the grip of an insatiable habit. As with alcohol, heavy dependence on cocaine and heroin is acquired over time.

Changing priorities

It is a reasonable concern that the disadvantaged would be most vulnerable in a system where drugs are cheap and legally available. But the poor are also the ones paying the heaviest price for prohibition. Most drug users are not poor minorities, but these groups are most affected by the illegal drug trade. "Each of our inner cities has become a bloody Bosnia," writes David Morrison, the journalist and former addict. "But who with the power to make a difference really gives a damn? Having decamped for the suburbs, the middle classes don't have to see the dreadful damage done."

Of course, lifting prohibition would not be a panacea for our most troubled communities. But imagine the benefits of cutting out the black market. Profit would be eliminated from the drug trade, which means kids wouldn't be drawn to dealing, addicts wouldn't be pushed to thieving, and the sea of violence and crime would ebb. Innocent kids like Launice Smith wouldn't be caught in the crossfire. Students like Jovan Rogers, who survived the drug trade and returned to school, would be less likely to drop out in the first place. And the intense marketing efforts of drug dealers in schoolyards and hallways would stop. (As it stands, dealers encourage users however they can—the more addicts, the more profits for them.)

Meanwhile, police could focus on real crime—and they'd have the prison space to lock up violent or repeat offenders. Businesses, now scared off by inner-city crime, might be drawn back into these communities, and a cycle of recovery could begin. For drug addicts, the federal government could spend the billions now wasted on law enforcement and interdiction to provide effective treatment.

At the same time, the government could clamp down on the alcohol and cigarette corporate behemoths, and make sure that such they never get their hands on now-illegal drugs by controlling distribution through package stores—displaying warnings in the stores and on containers themselves. Advertising and marketing, clearly, would be prohibited and government would also have to fund an intensive campaign of public education to prevent misuse, abuse, and addiction.

Beyond government, we must recognize as a culture the damage done by drugs—even if we accept the rights of individuals to use them. The entertainment industry should take this responsibility very seriously. As it is, the scare tactics used by the government give even greater currency to Hollywood's images of the hip, outlaw drug user.

After so many years of prohibition—and a vociferous government effort to distort the truth—it's not hard to imagine why people would fear an epidemic of new drug addicts after prohibition. But such fears are exaggerated. The increase in use could be kept to a minimum by smart public policy. Meanwhile, we would be undoing the horror of present policy—which fractures communities, leaves kids scared to go to the playground, and pushes young men toward death or jail.

With reforms, we could stop this great damage. The good, almost certainly, would far overshadow the new problems created. Isn't it a moral imperative that we at least try? If legalization proves to be a failure—though the best evidence indicates it would not—we could return to present policy, or find a third way.

Many may be tempted to split the difference—maintain prohibition, but ease some of the penalties. Or legalize the mildest of the illegal drugs, such as marijuana. Or make drugs available to addicts by prescription. There's nothing to prevent experimenting with different strategies. But remember, the tighter the restrictions, the more fuel to the fire of the black market. Undermining the black market has to be the principle of any reform.

The other temptation is to justify the costs of prohibition in moral terms—"drugs are evil." But pining for a "drug-free America" doesn't change the reality that we'll never have one. Even Lee Brown concedes that the best he can do—with a budget approaching $15 billion dollars—is reduce drug use by 5 percent annually. Is dissuading a few hundred thousand marijuana users worth the terror of the black market?

Ultimately drug policy does come down to tradeoffs. The simple truth is that humans are tempted by intoxicants. And, in a free society like ours, the rights of life and liberty will always be accompanied by people pursuing stiff drinks, or lines of cocaine, or marijuana cigarettes. Inflating the price of drugs through prohibition and jailing sellers and users of drugs sprang from a noble sentiment—that we could eliminate the scourge of addiction, or limit it significantly. Now we know that the enormous efforts in law enforcement have yielded few benefits in curbing drug abuse—and are a paltry disincentive for many drug users and would-be users. The prohibition experiment has failed. The time has come to recognize the great harm it has done. The United States is now akin to a person with poison ivy, scratching furiously at the rashes, and holding fast in denial when they do not go away: Soon, the blood begins to flow. These wounds show themselves every day, in brutal murders and bleak urban landscapes.

We will always have a "drug problem" of some sort. The question is: What *kind* of drug problem? Ultimately, choosing between regulation and prohibition turns on a simple question: Is it better to allow some individuals to make a bad choice, or to subject many, many innocent people to drive-by shootings, rampant crime, and dangerous schools? The moral policy is to protect the innocent—and then do our best to help the others as well.

3

Legalization of Drugs Would Increase Violent Crime

James A. Inciardi and Christine A. Saum

James A. Inciardi is a professor in the Department of Sociology and Criminal Justice at the University of Delaware, in Newark and is director of the university's Center for Drug and Alcohol Studies. Inciardi is also co-editor of The American Drug Scene. *Christine A. Saum is a doctoral candidate and a research associate at the Center for Drug and Alcohol Studies who coauthored* Cocaine-Exposed Infants: Social, Legal, and Public Health Issues *with Inciardi and Hilary Suratt.*

Those who support the legalization of drugs argue that legalization would reduce drug-related crime. Research reveals, however, that legalization would likely increase rather than decrease violent crime. The argument that violence is the result of criminalizing the drug trade ignores the research that shows that drugs themselves make users violent. Because legalization would likely create more users, legalization would also increase violent crime. The argument that legalization would reduce crime related to compulsive use of drugs is also faulty because research shows that many who use drugs are involved in crime before they begin to use drugs.

Frustrated by the government's apparent inability to reduce the supply of illegal drugs on the streets of America, and disquieted by media accounts of innocents victimized by drug-related violence, some policy makers are convinced that the "war on drugs" has failed. In an attempt to find a better solution to the "drug crisis" or, at the very least, to try an alternative strategy, they have proposed legalizing drugs.

They argue that, if marijuana, cocaine, heroin, and other drugs were legalized, several positive things would probably occur: (1) drug prices would fall; (2) users would obtain their drugs at low, government-regulated prices, and they would no longer be forced to resort to crime in order to support their habits, (3) levels of drug-related crime, and particularly violent crime, would significantly decline, resulting in less crowded courts, jails, and prisons (this would allow law-enforcement personnel to focus their

Reprinted from James A. Inciardi and Christine A. Saum, "Legalization Madness," *The Public Interest*, Spring 1996. Reprinted with permission from James A. Inciardi.

energies on the "real criminals" in society); and (4) drug production, distribution, and sale would no longer be controlled by organized crime, and thus such criminal syndicates as the Colombian cocaine "cartels," the Jamaican "posses," and the various "mafias" around the country and the world would be decapitalized, and the violence associated with drug distribution rivalries would be eliminated.

Research has documented that chronic users of amphetamines, methamphetamine, and cocaine in particular tend to exhibit hostile and aggressive behaviors.

By contrast, the anti-legalization camp argues that violent crime would not necessarily decline in a legalized drug market. In fact, there are three reasons why it might actually increase. First, removing the criminal sanctions against the possession and distribution of illegal drugs would make them more available and attractive and, hence, would create large numbers of new users. Second, an increase in use would lead to a greater number of dysfunctional addicts who could not support themselves, their habits, or their lifestyles through legitimate means. Hence crime would be their only alternative. Third, more users would mean more of the violence associated with the ingestion of drugs.

These divergent points of view tend to persist because the relationships between drugs and crime are quite complex and because the possible outcomes of a legalized drug market are based primarily on speculation. However, it is possible, from a careful review of the existing empirical literature on drugs and violence, to make some educated inferences.

Considering "legalization"

Yet much depends upon what we mean by "legalizing drugs." Would all currently illicit drugs be legalized or would the experiment be limited to just certain ones? True legalization would be akin to selling such drugs as heroin and cocaine on the open market, much like alcohol and tobacco, with a few age-related restrictions. In contrast, there are "medicalization" and "decriminalization" alternatives. Medicalization approaches are of many types, but, in essence, they would allow users to obtain prescriptions for some, or all, currently illegal substances. Decriminalization removes the criminal penalties associated with the possession of small amounts of illegal drugs for personal use, while leaving intact the sanctions for trafficking, distribution, and sale.

But what about crack-cocaine? A quick review of the literature reveals that the legalizers, the decriminalizers, and the medicalizers avoid talking about this particular form of cocaine. Perhaps they do not want to legalize crack out of fear of the drug itself, or of public outrage. Arnold S. Trebach, a professor of law at American University and president of the Drug Policy Foundation, is one of the very few who argues for the full legalization of all drugs, including crack. He explains, however, that most are reluctant to discuss the legalization of crack-cocaine because, "it is a very dangerous drug. . . . I know that for many people the very thought of making crack legal destroys any inclination they might have had for even thinking about drug-law reform."

There is a related concern associated with the legalization of cocaine. Because crack is easily manufactured from powder cocaine (just add water and baking soda and cook on a stove or in a microwave), many drug-policy reformers hold that no form of cocaine should be legalized. But this weakens the argument that legalization will reduce drug-related violence, for much of this violence would appear to be in the cocaine- and crack-distribution markets.

To better understand the complex relationship between drugs and violence, we will discuss the data in the context of three models developed by Paul J. Goldstein of the University of Illinois at Chicago. They are the "psychopharmacological," "economically compulsive," and "systemic" explanations of violence. The first model holds, correctly in our view, that some individuals may become excitable, irrational, and even violent due to the ingestion of specific drugs. In contrast, taking a more economic approach to the behavior of drug users, the second holds that some drug users engage in violent crime mainly for the sake of supporting their drug use. The third model maintains that drug-related violent crime is simply the result of the drug market under a regime of illegality.

Psychopharmacological violence

The case for legalization rests in part upon the faulty assumption that drugs themselves do not cause violence; rather, so goes the argument, violence is the result of depriving drug addicts of drugs or of the "criminal" trafficking in drugs. But, as researcher Barry Spunt points out, "Users of drugs do get violent when they get high."

Research has documented that chronic users of amphetamines, methamphetamine, and cocaine in particular tend to exhibit hostile and aggressive behaviors. Psychopharmacological violence can also be a product of what is known as "cocaine psychosis." As dose and duration of cocaine use increase, the development of cocaine-related psychopathology is not uncommon. Cocaine psychosis is generally preceded by a transitional period characterized by increased suspiciousness, compulsive behavior, fault finding, and eventually paranoia. When the psychotic state is reached, individuals may experience visual, as well as auditory, hallucinations, with persecutory voices commonly heard. Many believe that they are being followed by police or that family, friends, and others are plotting against them.

Moreover, everyday events are sometimes misinterpreted by cocaine users in ways that support delusional beliefs. When coupled with the irritability and hyperactivity that cocaine tends to generate in almost all of its users, the cocaine-induced paranoia may lead to violent behavior as a means of "self-defense" against imagined persecutors. The violence associated with cocaine psychosis is a common feature in many crack houses across the United States. Violence may also result from the irritability associated with drug-withdrawal syndromes. In addition, some users ingest drugs before committing crimes to both loosen inhibitions and bolster their resolve to break the law.

Acts of violence may result from either periodic or chronic use of a drug. For example, in a study of drug use and psychopathy among Baltimore City jail inmates, researchers at the University of Baltimore reported that cocaine use was related to irritability, resentment, hostility, and assault. They concluded that these indicators of aggression may be a function of drug effects rather than of a predisposition to these behaviors. Similarly, Barry Spunt and his colleagues at National Development and Research Institutes (NDRI) in New York City found that of 269 convicted murderers incarcerated in New York State prisons, 45 percent were high at the time of the offense. Three in 10 believed that the homicide was related to their drug use, challenging conventional beliefs that violence only infrequently occurs as a result of drug consumption.

A great many of the victims of homicide and other forms of violence are drinkers and drug users themselves.

Even marijuana, which pro-legalizers consider harmless, may have a connection with violence and crime. Spunt and his colleagues attempted to determine the role of marijuana in the crimes of the homicide offenders they interviewed in the New York State prisons. One-third of those who had ever used marijuana had smoked the drug in the 24-hour period prior to the homicide. Moreover, 31 percent of those who considered themselves to be "high" at the time of committing murder felt that the homicide and marijuana were related. William Blount of the University of South Florida interviewed abused women in prisons and shelters for battered women located throughout Florida. He and his colleagues found that 24 percent of those who killed their abusers were marijuana users while only 8 percent of those who did not kill their abusers smoked marijuana.

The problem of alcohol abuse

A point that needs emphasizing is that alcohol, because it is legal, accessible, and inexpensive, is linked to violence to a far greater extent than any illegal drug. For example, in the study just cited, it was found that an impressive 64 percent of those women who eventually killed their abusers were alcohol users (44 percent of those who did not kill their abusers were alcohol users). Indeed, the extent to which alcohol is responsible for violent crimes in comparison with other drugs is apparent from the statistics. For example, Carolyn Block and her colleagues at the Criminal Justice Information Authority in Chicago found that, between 1982 and 1989, the use of alcohol by offenders or victims in local homicides ranged from 18 percent to 32 percent.

Alcohol has, in fact, been consistently linked to homicide. Spunt and his colleagues interviewed 268 homicide offenders incarcerated in New York State correctional facilities to determine the role of alcohol in their crimes: Thirty-one percent of the respondents reported being drunk at the time of the crime and 19 percent believed that the homicide was related to their drinking. More generally, Douglass Murdoch of Quebec's McGill

University found that in some 9,000 criminal cases drawn from a multinational sample, 62 percent of violent offenders were drinking shortly before, or at the time of, the offense.

It appears that alcohol reduces the inhibitory control of threat, making it more likely that a person will exhibit violent behaviors normally suppressed by fear. In turn, this reduction of inhibition heightens the probability that intoxicated persons will perpetrate, or become victims of, aggressive behavior.

When analyzing the psychopharmacological model of drugs and violence, most of the discussions focus on the offender and the role of drugs in causing or facilitating crime. But what about the victims? Are the victims of drug- and alcohol-related homicides simply casualties of someone else's substance abuse? In addressing these questions, the data demonstrates that victims are likely to be drug users as well. For example, in an analysis of the 4,298 homicides that occurred in New York City during 1990 and 1991, Kenneth Tardiff of Cornell University Medical College found that the victims of these offenses were 10 to 50 times more likely to be cocaine users than were members of the general population. Of the white female victims, 60 percent in the 25- to 34-year age group had cocaine in their systems; for black females, the figure was 72 percent. Tardiff speculated that the classic symptoms of cocaine use—irritability, paranoia, aggressiveness—may have instigated the violence. In another study of cocaine users in New York City, female high-volume users were found to be victims of violence far more frequently than low-volume and nonusers of cocaine. Studies in numerous other cities and countries have yielded the same general findings—that a great many of the victims of homicide and other forms of violence are drinkers and drug users themselves.

Economically compulsive violence

Supporters of the economically compulsive model of violence argue that in a legalized market, the prices of "expensive drugs" would decline to more affordable levels, and, hence, predatory crimes would become unnecessary. This argument is based on several specious assumptions. First, it assumes that there is empirical support for what has been referred to as the "enslavement theory of addiction." Second, it assumes that people addicted to drugs commit crimes only for the purpose of supporting their habits. Third, it assumes that, in a legalized market, users could obtain as much of the drugs as they wanted whenever they wanted. Finally, it assumes that, if drugs are inexpensive, they will be affordable, and thus crime would be unnecessary.

With respect to the first premise, there has been for the better part of this century a concerted belief among many in the drug-policy field that addicts commit crimes because they are "enslaved" to drugs, and further that, because of the high price of heroin, cocaine, and other illicit chemicals on the black market, users are forced to commit crimes in order to support their drug habits. However, there is no solid empirical evidence to support this contention. From the 1920s through the end of the 1960s, hundreds of studies of the relationship between crime and addiction were conducted. Invariably, when one analysis would support the posture of "enslavement theory," the next would affirm the view that addicts were criminals first and that their drug use was but one more manifestation of their deviant lifestyles. In retrospect, the difficulty lay in the ways that many of the studies had been conducted: Biases and deficiencies in research designs and sampling had rendered their findings of little value.

Studies since the mid 1970s of active drug users on the streets of New York, Miami, Baltimore, and elsewhere have demonstrated that the "enslavement theory" has little basis in reality. All of these studies of the criminal careers of drug users have convincingly documented that, while drug use tends to intensify and perpetuate criminal behavior, it usually does not initiate criminal careers. In fact, the evidence suggests that among the majority of street drug users who are involved in crime, their criminal careers are well established prior to the onset of either narcotics or cocaine use. As such, it would appear that the "inference of causality"—that the high price of drugs on the black market itself causes crime—is simply false.

Among the majority of street drug users who are involved in crime, their criminal careers are well established prior to the onset of either narcotics or cocaine use.

Looking at the second premise, a variety of studies show that addicts commit crimes for reasons other than supporting their drug habit. They do so also for daily living expenses. For example, researchers at the Center for Drug and Alcohol Studies at the University of Delaware who studied crack users on the streets of Miami found that, of the active addicts interviewed, 85 percent of the male and 70 percent of the female interviewees paid for portions of their living expenses through street crime. In fact, one-half of the men and one-fourth of the women paid for 90 percent or more of their living expenses through crime. And, not surprisingly, 96 percent of the men and 99 percent of the women had not held a legal job in the 90-day period before being interviewed for the study.

With respect to the third premise, that in a legalized market users could obtain as much of the drugs as they wanted whenever they wanted, only speculation is possible. More than likely, however, there would be some sort of regulation, and hence black markets for drugs would persist for those whose addictions were beyond the medicalized or legalized allotments. In a decriminalized market, levels of drug-related violence would likely either remain unchanged or increase (if drug use increased).

As for the last premise, that cheap drugs preclude the need to commit crimes to obtain them, the evidence emphatically suggests that this is not the case. Consider crack-cocaine: Although crack "rocks" are available on the illegal market for as little as two dollars in some locales, users are still involved in crime-driven endeavors to support their addictions. For example, researchers Norman S. Miller and Mark S. Gold surveyed 200 consecutive callers to the 1-800-COCAINE hotline who considered themselves to have a problem with crack. They found that, despite the low cost of crack, 63 percent of daily users and 40 percent of non-daily users spent more than $200 per week on the drug. Similarly, interviews conducted by NDRI researchers in New York City with almost 400 drug users contacted in the streets, jails, and treatment programs revealed that almost one-half of them spent over $1,000 a month on crack. The study also documented that crack users—despite the low cost of their drug of choice—spent more money on drugs than did users of heroin, powder cocaine, marijuana, and alcohol.

Systemic violence

It is the supposed systemic violence associated with trafficking in cocaine and crack in America's inner cities that has received the attention of drug-policy critics interested in legalizing drugs. Certainly it might appear that, if heroin and cocaine were legal substances, systemic drug-related violence would decline. However, there are two very important questions in this regard: First, is drug-related violence more often psychopharmacological or systemic? Second, is the great bulk of systemic violence related to the distribution of crack? If most of the drug-related violence is psychopharmacological in nature, and if systemic violence is typically related to crack—the drug generally excluded from consideration when legalization is recommended—then legalizing drugs would probably not reduce violent crime.

Regarding the first question, several studies conducted in New York City tend to contradict, or at least not support, the notion that legalizing drugs would reduce violent, systemic-related crime. For example, Paul J. Goldstein's ethnographic studies of male and female drug users during the late 1980s found that cocaine-related violence was more often psychopharmacological than systemic. Similarly, Kenneth Tardiff's study of 4,298 New York City homicides found that 31 percent of the victims had used cocaine in the 24-hour period prior to their deaths. One of the conclusions of the study was that the homicides were not necessarily related to drug dealing. In all likelihood, as victims of homicide, the cocaine users may have provoked violence through their irritability, paranoid thinking, and verbal or physical aggression—all of which are among the psychopharmacological effects of cocaine.

> *Crack users—despite the low cost of their drug of choice—spend more money on drugs than did users of heroin, powder cocaine, marijuana, and alcohol.*

Regarding the second question, the illegal drug most associated with systemic violence is crack-cocaine. Of all illicit drugs, crack is the one now responsible for the most homicides. In a study done in New York City in 1988 by Goldstein and his colleagues, crack was found to be connected with 32 percent of all homicides and 60 percent of all drug-related homicides. Furthermore, although there is evidence that crack sellers are more violent than other drug sellers, this violence is not confined to the drug-selling context—violence potentials appear to precede involvement in selling.

Thus, though crack has been blamed for increasing violence in the marketplace, this violence actually stems from the psychopharmacological consequences of crack use. Ansley Hamid, a professor of anthropology at the John Jay College of Criminal Justice in New York, reasons that increases in crack-related violence are due to the deterioration of informal and formal social controls throughout communities that have been destabilized by economic processes and political decisions. If this is the case, does anyone really believe that we can improve these complex social problems through the simple act of legalizing drugs?

Don't just say no

The issue of whether or not legalization would create a multitude of new users also needs to be addressed. It has been shown that many people do not use drugs simply because drugs are illegal. As Mark A.R. Kleiman, author of *Against Excess: Drug Policy for Results*, recently put it: Illegality by itself tends to suppress consumption, independent of its effect on price, both because some consumers are reluctant to disobey the law and because illegal products are harder to find and less reliable as to quality and labeling than legal ones."

Although there is no way of accurately estimating how many new users there would be if drugs were legalized, there would probably be many. To begin with, there is the historical example of Prohibition. During Prohibition, there was a decrease of 20 percent to 50 percent in the number of alcoholics. These estimates were calculated based on a decline in cirrhosis and other alcohol-related deaths; after Prohibition ended, both of these indicators increased.

Currently, relatively few people are steady users of drugs. The University of Michigan's *Monitoring the Future* study reported in 1995 that only two-tenths of 1 percent of high-school seniors are daily users of either hallucinogens, cocaine, heroin, sedatives, or inhalants. It is the addicts who overwhelmingly consume the bulk of the drug supply—80 percent of all alcohol and almost 100 percent of all heroin. In other words, there are significantly large numbers of non-users who have yet to even try drugs, let alone use them regularly. Of those who begin to use drugs "recreationally," researchers estimate that approximately 10 percent go on to serious, heavy, chronic, compulsive use. Herbert Kleber, the former deputy director of the Office of National Drug Control Policy, recently estimated that cocaine legalization might multiply the number of addicts from the current 2 million to between 18 and 50 million (which are the estimated numbers of problem drinkers and nicotine addicts).

This suggests that drug prohibition seems to be having some very positive effects and that legalizing drugs would not necessarily have a depressant effect on violent crime. With legalization, violent crime would likely escalate; or perhaps some types of systemic violence would decline at the expense of greatly increasing the overall rate of violent crime. Moreover, legalizing drugs would likely increase physical illnesses and compound any existing psychiatric problems among users and their family members. And finally, legalizing drugs would not eliminate the effects of unemployment, inadequate housing, deficient job skills, economic worries, and physical abuse that typically contribute to the use of drugs.

4

Laws Against Drugs
Protect Society

Barry R. McCaffrey

Barry R. McCaffrey, a retired four star general in the U.S. Army, was confirmed by the U.S. Senate as the Director of the White House Office of National Drug Control Policy on February 29, 1996. He is also a member of the National Security Council and the Cabinet Council on Counternarcotics.

The United States has had a long history of opposition to dangerous drugs. The Food and Drug Act of 1906 protected consumers from unsafe medicines, the Opium Exclusion Act of 1909 banned opium, and public outrage resulted in the censorship of drug use in movies. America has entered a new phase in its history of dealing with drugs. Crack cocaine is destroying inner cities, but drug use also has invaded suburban and rural areas. Not only do drugs damage the minds and bodies of the young, but the international drug trade uses profits from drug smuggling to finance arms deals. Drug laws are therefore necessary to protect American citizens.

It is an honor to address this distinguished forum, founded in 1903 by the editorial writer of the San Francisco Chronicle. As a service club where men and women could debate issues of public concern, the Commonwealth Club sponsored talks on a wide range of topics, many of which led to social change and government legislation. For nine decades, noted national and international leaders have aired their concerns here. Among those speakers were Teddy Roosevelt, Harry Truman, Martin Luther King Jr., Robert Kennedy, Desmond Tutu, George Bush, and Bill Clinton. Authors honored by the Commonwealth Club Book Awards included John Steinbeck, Irving Stone, and Leon Uris, to name just a few. The advent of radio and television have now extended the reach of these talks beyond California to embrace a national audience.

In light of this ninety-four-year tradition of intellectual discourse, let me suggest that we begin our consideration of illegal drugs today with an historical analysis of this problem. Calls for legalization as the panacea for

Reprinted from Barry R. McCaffrey, "National Drug Control: Reducing Drug Use and Its Consequences in America," a speech delivered to the Commonwealth Club, San Francisco, CA, July 2, 1997.

the nation's drug ills should be viewed with the skepticism borne of American historical experience. The tendency to forget much of America's experience with addictive substances goes to the very nature of drugs and the culture they spawn. A drugged society suffers from long-term memory loss to the point of amnesia.

The lure of illegal drugs involves a desire for intense pleasure and instant reward. Drug users crave out-of-body joy and peace at the drop of a pill, in a few breaths, or within minutes of injection. Lost in the self and the present, the person on drugs is neither preparing for the future nor learning from the past. The drug culture nods in the now; its orientation is historical. Yet history has much to teach us about the problems of substance abuse, which we ignore at our peril.

A history of rejecting dangerous drugs

America's confrontation with dangerous drugs dates back to the nineteenth century when over-the-counter syrups were heavily laced with morphine; Coca-Cola and other beverages contained cocaine; and Bayer Pharmaceutical Products introduced heroin—touted as non-addictive and sold without prescription (one year before Bayer offered aspirin). At the turn of the century, opium dens catered to communities throughout the United States. We do not have to speculate about what would happen if addictive drugs were legal without prescription. Our country has already tried that route, suffered, and roundly rejected the scourge of drugs on our communities, schools, work places, and families.

By popular demand, the Food and Drug Act of 1906 required that all ingredients in products and medicines be revealed to consumers, many of whom had become addicted to substances falsely marketed as safe. In 1909, the Smoking Opium Exclusion Act banned the importation of smokable opium—providing the first national antidrug legislation. Five years later, the Harrison Narcotic Act implemented even broader and more effective drug control laws. In 1911, the first International Conference on Opium convened in the Hague to control narcotics trafficking. By the 1920s, doctors in America were prohibited from prescribing opiates for non-medical purposes, including the treatment of addicts.

Our country has already tried [legalization], suffered, and roundly rejected the scourge of drugs on our communities, schools, workplaces, and families.

Problems with cocaine addiction plagued Hollywood in the 20s to the point where movie mogul Louis B. Mayer complained: "If this keeps up, there won't be any motion picture industry." In response to public outrage over depictions of drug use in film, thirty-seven states passed censorship bills by 1922. The drug problem did not first hit the United States in the 1960s, as many Americans believe. An earlier drug epidemic raged between 1885 and 1925, followed by a resurgence from 1950 to 1970, when heroin poured into America from Turkey by way of France. Ten years later, a third and incredibly destructive wave of drug abuse brought havoc to our shores as Colombian cartels flooded our streets with cocaine.

Underestimating the hazards of drug use

The tendency to underestimate the hazards of drug use has been made in successive generations. We forget what has been painfully demonstrated in years past. The seductive quality of drugs over the years has continued to fool many professionals and laymen. The father of modern psychiatry, Sigmund Freud, initially thought cocaine was non-addictive and relatively harmless—a mistake made in the mid-1880s that was repeated nearly a hundred years later. Leading universities hosted professors infatuated with psychedelics in the 1960s and 70's—or stimulants and narcotics in the 80's and 90's.

Many physicians and researchers have grossly underestimated drug dangers. Dr. Morris Manges of Mount Sinai Hospital wrote, in an 1898 issue of the New York Medical Journal, about treating coughs with heroin: apparently, there was no habituation to the drug. By 1900, Manges released a second glowing report for heroin based on a survey of 141 doctors. The author noted only a small number of cases where addiction was observed. But three years later, Dr. George Pettey voiced unequivocal alarm in The Heroin Habit: Another Curse, published in the Alabama Medical Journal. Pettey realized that heroin produced what is for all intents and purposes the opium habit.

With respect to cocaine, the absence of heroin-type withdrawal symptoms tricked some researchers into missing this drug's addictive quality, which is based on reward, according to Dr. Robert Dupont, a former head of the National Institute of Drug Abuse. In 1979, Dr. Robert Byck of Yale Medical School warned about the devastation caused by smoked coca paste used in Peru—this before crack ominously captured so many Americans. Wooed into a false sense of security by the supposed benign quality of smoked marijuana, unwitting victims of crack cocaine wrongly concluded that smoking this substance—unlike injecting—would be a safe route of administration. (Dr. David Musto highlights a parallel misconception a century earlier when physicians and patients alike mistakenly concluded that the use of a syringe with pure morphine, which reduced the quantity of drugs needed to produce the same effect, would limit rather than expand the likelihood of addiction.) Actually, crack cocaine made heroin look like the good old days, according to historian Dr. Jill Jonnes. The advent of crack houses and crack babies (the NIDA National Pregnancy and Health Survey estimated 1 to 2 percent of American infants in 1992 had been exposed to cocaine in utero) marked a new and terrible stage in the history of drug abuse.

In 1986—the same year that the military reported cutting drug use by half—the deaths of Len Bias, [a basketball player], and Don Rogers, [a football player] demonstrated to the public that one dose of cocaine could prove lethal even to healthy young athletes. Had anyone bothered to consult the research, they would have discovered that this fatal syndrome was identified decades ago. In addition, the historical experience of cultures as different as China, Egypt, and Japan confirmed that no society could prosper while tolerating addictive drugs.

The cost of drug use

Drug use cannot be considered in a vacuum. We must understand it within the context of crime, violence, corruption, prostitution, multinational cartels, adverse health consequences, enormous social costs, and the collapse of our cities. Drug use is not limited to one area of the country or social class but permeates suburban and rural areas as well as urban locations. On an international scale, narco-terrorists use the illegal drug trade as a means to other ends. Arms deals fueled by drug capital are part of the deal. On the other side of the drug register are young consumers. Youth are particularly vulnerable to the allure of drugs and to the damage toxic substances cause developing bodies and minds.

The drug problem has personal and psychological dimensions. However, it is also a social, medical, communal, economic, and global problem that involves larger systems—beginning with the family and reaching to the nation and hemisphere. What is the effect of addictive drugs on inner cities where alternate routes to professional achievement, wealth, insight, experience, travel, satisfaction, fulfillment, and creativity are less abundant than on college campuses?

The problem of addictive drugs is complicated by criminal syndicates and multinational rings that procure these substances. Over international crime, neither individuals nor neighborhoods wield significant power. Many countries have lost control in the face of such opponents. Therefore, we must use the federal government and international cooperation to protect our citizens.

From seat belts to sewage disposal, America has used the law to protect citizens.

Born of revolution only two centuries ago, America has been a forward-thinking, optimistic country oriented toward the present and future. In an age of electronic communication and computers, instant transmission of information compounds the tendency to value what is news right now as opposed to yesterday. But ignorance of the past condemns us to repeat errors unnecessarily. An antidote to arrogance, memory is the key to education and collective progress. The history of illegal drugs informs the present.

Illegal drugs are a byproduct of an industrial society that has led us to tamper—for better and for worse—with the body's inner environment. The United States has one of the worst addiction problems of any country in the developed world in part because of our wealth. We must focus our resources, including the intelligence of our greatest minds, to solve this problem. We can lead the world in controlling illegal drugs—primarily through prevention and treatment—just as we made great strides in guarding consumer safety and cleaning up the outer environment. From seat belts to sewage disposal, America has used the law to protect citizens. The struggle against the danger of drug abuse is another such effort. We must free all people trapped in the physical and spiritual misery of compulsive drug addiction.

5

Prohibition of Drugs
Is Unconstitutional

Paul Hager

Paul Hager is a software engineer and developer in Indianapolis, Indiana and member of the Libertarian Party. His position on the legalization of drugs has been part of his 1996 and 1998 congressional campaigns and his reports to the Indiana Civil Liberties Union.

The U.S. Constitution specifically grants certain powers to the federal government, and all other powers are reserved for the states. No amendment grants the federal government power to restrict drugs, yet the government encourages the myth of rising crime and drug use to justify its interference in these matters. Alcohol and tobacco are more addictive and the consumption of alcohol often promotes violence, yet unlike other drugs, these substances are not prohibited. The attempt to prohibit alcohol during the 1920s and '30s led to an increase in homicides, alcohol use, and the number of young people involved in crime, not unlike the modern-day attempts to prohibit drugs.

On the national political scene, the issue of crime is a perennial favorite among the Republican and Democratic politicians. They can be counted on to make extravagant promises to "solve" the "crime problem" by "swift," "forceful," (choose appropriate dynamic metaphor) legislative action. Enacting legislation is certainly something that they can do and much effort goes into "crime bills" and "terrorism bills" which create new categories of federal crime and expand the federal reach into areas formerly reserved to state and local governments. In the midst of all of this legislative activity, there is literally no national politician who questions any of this. The most basic question that needs to be asked is where does Congress get the power to pass these laws? In fact, a compelling case can be made that much of what Congress does in the area of crime legislation violates fundamental principles of federalism that are embodied in the U.S. Constitution and spelled out in the 10th Amendment.

For some, the issue of constitutionality will be beside the point. After

Reprinted from Paul Hager, "Crime and the Drug War: The Politics of Hysteria," *The Libertarian Corner*, 1996, available at www.cs.indiana.edu/hyplan/hagerp/drugwar.html. Reprinted with permission from the author.

all, much of the Constitution is over 200 years old and "out of step" with the problems of modern society. This is certainly a position articulated by President Bill Clinton. Of course, just ignoring the Constitution is not the correct way of going about things, but it could be amended to give Congress any power society deems necessary to fight the "rising tide of crime." Here, too, questions can be asked, the most pertinent being: is there actually a seriously escalating rate of crime in our society? As it turns out, contrary to the statements of politicians, it can be conclusively shown that the crime rate is not rising and the "emergency" that is being used to justify Congressional action doesn't exist.

The crime rate is not rising and the "emergency" that is being used to justify Congressional action doesn't exist.

Even the demonstration that a crime emergency doesn't exist may not be enough for some people. Crime may not be rising but it is still too high, they would say. I don't disagree with that statement. In fact, I offer the only rational legislative strategy that can have a measurable impact in reducing crime in America.

In the sections that follow I will address the questions I have raised and state my solution.

The unconstitutional war

The U.S. Constitution is the document that lays out the basic form of the national government and enumerates the specific powers it may exercise. The powers of Congress — the kinds of laws it may pass or agencies it may create — are listed in Article I, Section 8. The powers that the national government exercises have been delegated by the several states — they retain all other powers. The powers retained by the states include the passage and enforcement of criminal laws, such as laws against theft, assault, and murder. Nowhere in the Constitution has Congress been given the power to legislate in this area.

Some may claim that the "general welfare clause" at the beginning of Section 8 and the "necessary and proper" clause at the end give Congress broad powers to do anything it wants. While seemingly plausible, this argument is ultimately unsupportable. In fact, one of the objections to ratifying the Constitution made by the Anti-federalists was over just this point. The Federalists answered the objection in two ways.

The Federalists' first response to the objection was that the Anti-federalists had misconstrued the language of Section 8. The "general welfare" clause was merely a statement of purpose which the enumeration that followed explained. It was, in fact, essentially the same language used in the Articles of Confederation where it was a similar statement of purpose. This argument was most effectively made by James Madison in Federalist Number 41.

The second response grew out of the Anti-federalists' demand for a Bill of Rights. Although the Federalists initially argued that, given the constitutional framework of enumerated powers, a Bill of Rights was unnecessary, even dangerous (see Alexander Hamilton in Federalist Number 84), it became clear that a compromise would be necessary if the Constitution was to be ratified. One of the amendments which was offered as part of this compromise was the one that eventually became Amendment 10, which reads as follows:

> The powers not delegated to the United States by the Constitution, nor prohibited by it to the States, are reserved to the States respectively, or to the people.

The 10th was intended to explicitly state that the powers exercised by the national government must be specifically enumerated in the Constitution with all other powers being retained by the states or the people. The administration of criminal justice is not addressed in the Constitution, therefore it is a power of the states.

So where then has Congress gotten the power to set up a national police force (the F.B.I.), and to get involved in the area of criminal justice? The answer is that it has gradually come about through the misconstrual of the commerce clause and the taxing power. The most obvious example of this is drug prohibition and the drug war. In 1919 it took a constitutional amendment, the 18th, for Congress to pass a law to prohibit the drug alcohol. There has never been a similar constitutional amendment to prohibit other drugs. Instead, the taxing power was first used to regulate—not prohibit—opiates and cocaine. By a series of carefully targeted prosecutions and results-oriented Supreme Court decisions over the next 20 years, the federal government eventually ended up with the "power" to prohibit drugs. But this power is not constitutional by any stretch of the imagination.

Although alcohol really is a dangerous drug, alcohol prohibition did much more harm than good.

Accretion of governmental power without the benefit of a constitutional grant is very dangerous. It means that the government is ignoring the Constitution and is becoming an end in itself. It means that other constitutional provisions can and will be ignored. We are already seeing this. Protections against unreasonable search and seizure (the 4th Amendment), self-incrimination and double jeopardy (the 5th Amendment), denial of counsel (the 6th Amendment), and unreasonable fines (the 8th Amendment) have all been substantially eroded in recent years in order to prosecute the drug war and stem the "rising tide of crime." Contempt for the Constitution in one area breeds contempt for the Constitution in all areas.

The dangerous myth of rising crime

Federal involvement in criminal justice is justified on the grounds that there is an epidemic of crime, that it is out of control and threatening the very fabric of society. Politicians vie with each other to construct the most lurid metaphors for the crime increase and elections turn on which politician has done the best job of describing the other as "soft on crime." All of this posturing about crime is totally at odds with what science tells us about crime in America: violent crime in the U.S. has been dropping for years and an individual's risk of being the victim of a violent crime is less now than it was in the mid-1970s.

It is not as though this information about crime is particularly arcane or otherwise unavailable to the people who make laws. In fact, any college undergraduate taking an introductory course in criminology will find it in standard texts on the subject. For example, Samuel Walker's very readable text, *Sense and Nonsense about Crime and Drugs: A Policy Guide*, 3rd edition (1994), talks about "the myth of the American crime wave":

> The news media constantly run stories about "soaring" crime rates. This characterization is inaccurate. The idea that violent crime is constantly rising is a myth. In fact, serious crime has been declining for over 15 years. The National Crime Survey's victimization data . . . indicate that robbery declined 17.2 percent between 1973 and 1991; rape fell by 11.6 percent; household burglary dropped by 42.1 percent. Violent crime against the elderly fell by 61 percent between 1974 and 1991. This is *one of the longest and most significant declines in the crime rate in American history* [emphasis in the original]. Much of the public hysteria about crime is misplaced.

As Walker notes, news media almost uniformly exaggerate the incidence of crime. (A notable exception is ABC journalist, John Stossel, whose one hour exposé, "Are We Scaring Ourselves to Death," dealt with the myth of rising crime.) While reasons could perhaps be offered for the news media's consistent failure to get the story right, it is hard to find any justification for elected representatives who parrot exactly the same line. Politicians in office, and those seeking office, should have at least a modicum of knowledge about the society they seek to govern. If they lack even the fundamental knowledge taught in an introductory college class, one must seriously question their competence to serve in positions of such responsibility.

During the time that the incidence of violent crime has been falling, public fear of being a crime victim has increased. This is not surprising because the only thing that the public ever hears is that crime is getting worse every day. This guarantees that crime will be an important political issue when election time rolls around. It also means that the public will be disposed to give their votes to candidates who make them feel more secure.

Candidates can allay the fears of the electorate and win their votes by promising "tougher" laws, giving "more power" to police (translation: trashing the Bill of Rights), and getting the federal government "more involved" in dealing with the "crime problem." This translates into bigger budgets for federal law enforcement agencies and more power and responsibility for the bureaucrats who administer them. What ultimately matters is not the underlying social reality, but what the public is made to believe the reality is. Fear, thus, is a valuable commodity for politicians and bureaucrats because it is the engine that funds big government programs.

The prohibition problem

Another example of fear mongering that has benefitted those wishing to get more funding and gain more power is the declaration of a war on drugs during the Reagan administration. In the late 1970s, during the Carter administration, all drug use, both legal and illegal began to decline. This decline began shortly after many states decriminalized marijuana. Several years into the decline, at a time when the Reagan administration was being criticized for Nancy Reagan's extravagances, the "Just say no" campaign, spearheaded by the First Lady, was unveiled. Over the next few years, millions of dollars were poured into advertising campaigns by groups like the Partnership for a Drug-Free America which resurrected outrageous, reefer madness-style campaigns against marijuana and led the public to believe that drug use was out of control. Meanwhile, drug use continued to decline.

Although the decline in drug use started with a relaxation of the drug laws, as the laws became more draconian, and more and more non-violent drug users began to be jailed, a funny thing happened: drug use started to go up. It would be facile, not to mention unscientific, to claim that drug use began to increase because of the drug war. However, it is very clear that if the purpose in reversing the policy of the 1970s—which was toward decriminalization and medical treatment of drug problems—was to further decrease drug use, it was a dismal failure from the standpoint of public policy. From the standpoint of enhancing bureaucratic power and winning elections however, the drug war was wildly successful for those who embraced it. Federal drug enforcement budgets increased by tenfold, and prisons began to fill with non-violent drug users. This mandated the need for more prisons to house the drug offenders which, in turn, required more funding. Today, the Clinton administration, which is branded by the Republicans as "soft on drugs," is spending record levels (over $14 billion) on the drug war.

At this point, one might say that the illegal drugs are so bad that even if the federal government initially mislead the public about drug use in order to wage its war, the current effort is nonetheless justified. By way of response, the following brief test is proffered.

> The psychopharmacological (effect of the drug on the brain and behavior) and public health effects of four drugs are going to be described. Please identify which are legal and which are illegal based upon the actual harm they do to society. Drug 1: kills around 600 per 100,000 users per year, is 90% addictive, and is not associated with violent behavior. Drug 2: kills around 75-100 per 100,000 users per year, is 10% to 15% addictive, and is psychopharmacologically associated with violent behavior and a sizeable percentage of violent crime in the U.S. Drug 3: kills at most 25 per 100,000 users per year, is 5% to 30% addictive (depending upon route of administration), and psychopharmacologically is only slightly associated with violent behavior. Drug 4: kills such a small proportion of its users that no numbers are available, is probably less than 5% addictive, and is not

associated with violent behavior. [Answers: Drug 1 is tobacco cigarettes, Drug 2 is alcohol, Drug 3 is cocaine (powder and crack), Drug 4 is marijuana.]

If prohibition makes sense from the public policy standpoint, it is pretty
obvious from the foregoing that the wrong drugs are being prohibited.

History amply demonstrates that, although alcohol really is a dangerous drug, alcohol prohibition did much more harm than good. There is
general agreement among scholars who have studied the effects of alcohol
prohibition that it was directly responsible for the rise of organized crime
in the U.S. (The subsequent activities of organized crime have been used
to justify greater and greater federal involvement in law enforcement.)
Homicide rates soared during alcohol prohibition as criminal gangs fought
over territory. More and more young people became involved in illegal activities because it was advantageous for bootleggers to use young people as
"mules" (that is, people who carry or otherwise deliver contraband). This
resulted in young people being killed in shoot-outs. It was the corruption
of youth and the kids being killed in gang wars that finally turned the public against alcohol prohibition, which ended in 1933. Shortly after the end
of alcohol prohibition, homicide rates plummeted—within a few years
they had dropped 40%. If there was a benefit observed with alcohol prohibition it was that fewer people used the drug. This benefit was illusory,
however. The amount of alcohol consumed actually increased because
the economics of prohibition decreed that booze should be more potent.
Thus, adverse health effects associated with alcohol use actually went up
during prohibition.

> *Federal involvement in the criminal justice area has
> no constitutional nor public policy basis.*

While it is true that opiates, cocaine, marijuana, and hallucinogens
are different from alcohol in terms of their psychopharmacology, all of
the evidence is that their continued prohibition is having exactly the
same effect on society today as alcohol prohibition had 70-odd years ago.
For example, economist Milton Friedman, looking at the effect the criminal black market in drugs is having on the homicide rate estimates that
it is responsible for at least 10,000 homicides each year. Criminologist Al-
fred Blumstein, past president of the American Society of Criminology
(1991–1992), notes that the criminal black market in crack cocaine is a
major component of the increase in homicides committed by youths ages
15–24 that occurred in the last half of the 1980s. The fact that many of
the victims were also young underscores the tragedy of drug prohibition.

Today's drug prohibition, like alcohol prohibition before it, is a major driver of violent crime and homicide. Because black market activities
are concentrated in big cities and because young African-American males
have the most to gain economically from the illicit drug trade, they are
most often the casualties in the war: the leading cause of death among
African-American males ages 15–24 is homicide. It is easy to see that drug
prohibition is racist in its operation.

In the foregoing sections, I have shown that federal involvement in the criminal justice area has no constitutional nor public policy basis. In fact, the federal government bears primary responsibility for the extent to which violent crime is a problem in the U.S., due to its continuing the unconstitutional policy of drug prohibition. If we were to end the drug war and re-legalize the currently illegal drugs, there is every reason to believe that we would very quickly see a major drop in the rate of violent crime and homicide. This is the only federal government approach to crime that is both constitutional and that will really work.

6

Drugs Should Be Made Controlled Substances

Gary E. Johnson

Gary E. Johnson is the Republican governor of the state of New Mexico and the first governor in the history of New Mexico to be elected to two four-year consecutive terms. Johnson is also the owner of his own construction company and an accomplished triathlete.

Many people have made a poor choice in using marijuana, but they do not belong in jail. Like alcohol and tobacco, drugs cause deaths, but people are not incarcerated for simply using alcohol and tobacco: The use of these substances is regulated, particularly as regards their accessibility by young people. Drugs are a bad choice and a handicap, but the money spent on the war on drugs would be better spent regulating, taxing, and controlling the $400-billion per year drug industry than incarcerating those who use drugs.

I am a "cost-benefit" analysis person. What's the cost and what's the benefit? A couple of things scream out as failing cost-benefit criteria. One is education. The other is the war on drugs. We are spending $50 billion a year to combat drugs. I'm talking about police, courts, and jails. For the amount of money that we're putting into it, I want to suggest, the war on drugs is an absolute failure. My "outrageous" hypothesis is that under a legalized scenario, we could actually hold drug use level or see it decline.

Sometimes people say to me, "Governor, I am absolutely opposed to your stand on drugs." I respond by asking them, "You're for drugs, you want to see kids use drugs?" Let me make something clear. I'm not pro-drug. I'm against drugs. Don't do drugs. Drugs are a real handicap. Don't do alcohol or tobacco, either. They are real handicaps.

There's another issue beyond cost-benefit criteria. Should you go to jail for using drugs? And I'm not talking about doing drugs and committing a crime or driving a car. Should you go to jail for simply doing drugs? I say no, you shouldn't. People ask me, "What do you tell kids?" Well, you tell the truth: that by legalizing drugs, we can control them, regulate and tax them.

Excerpted from Governor Gary E. Johnson, speech before the Cato Institute in Washington, D.C., October 5, 1999.

If we legalize drugs, we might have a healthier society. And you explain how that might take place. But you emphasize that drugs are a bad choice. Don't do drugs. But if you do, we're not going to throw you in jail for it.

New laws and problems

If drugs are legalized, there will be a whole new set of laws. Let me mention a few of them. Let's say you can't do drugs if you're under 21. You can't sell drugs to kids. I say employers should be able to discriminate against drug users. Employers should be able to conduct drug tests, and they should not have to comply with the Americans With Disabilities Act, [which prohibits employers from discrimination against those who have a history of addiction]. Do drugs and commit a crime? Make it like a gun. Enhance the penalty for the crime in the same way we do today with guns. Do drugs and drive? There should be a law similar to one we have now for driving under the influence of alcohol.

I propose that we redirect the $50 billion that we're spending (state and federal) on the old laws to enforce a new set of laws. Society would be transformed if law enforcement could focus on crimes other than drug use. Police could crack down on speeding violations, burglaries, and other offenses that law enforcement now lacks the opportunity to enforce.

If drugs are legalized, there will be a new set of problems, but they will have only about half the negative consequences. A legalization model will be a dynamic process that will be fine-tuned as we go along.

Does anybody want to press a button that would retroactively punish the 80 million Americans who have done illegal drugs over the years? I might point out that I'm one of those individuals. In running for my first term in office, I offered the fact that I had smoked marijuana. And the media were very quick to say, "Oh, so you experimented with marijuana?" "No," I said, "I smoked marijuana!" This is something I did, along with a lot of other people. I look back on it now, and I view drugs as a handicap. I stopped because it was a handicap. The same with drinking and tobacco. But did my friends and I belong in jail? I don't think that we should continue to lock up Americans because of bad choices.

And what about the bad choices regarding alcohol and tobacco? I've heard people say, "Governor, you're not comparing alcohol to drugs? You're not comparing tobacco to drugs?" I say, "Hell no! Alcohol killed 150,000 people last year. And I'm not talking about drinking and driving. I'm just talking about the health effects. The health effects of tobacco killed 450,000 people last year." I don't mean to be flippant, but I don't know of anybody ever dying from a marijuana overdose.

Controlling drug use

I understand that 2,000 to 3,000 people died in 1998 from abusing cocaine and heroine. If drugs were legalized, those deaths would go away, theoretically speaking, because they would no longer be counted as accidental. Instead, they'd be suicides, because in a legalized scenario drugs are controlled, taxed, and properly understood. I want to be so bold as to say that marijuana is never going to have the devastating effects on society that alcohol has had.

My own informal poll among doctors reveals that 75–80 percent of the patients they examine have health-related problems due to alcohol and tobacco. My brother is a cardiothoracic surgeon who performs heart transplants. He says that 80 percent of the problems he sees are alcohol and tobacco related. He sees about six people a year who have infected heart valves because of intravenous drug use, but the infection isn't from the drugs themselves. It's the dirty needles that cause the health problems.

Marijuana is said to be a gateway drug. We all know that, right? You're 85 times more likely to do cocaine if you do marijuana. I don't mean to be flippant, but 100 percent of all substance abuse starts with milk. You've heard it, but that bears repeating. My new mantra here is "Just Say Know." Just know that there are two sides to all these arguments. I think the facts boil down to drugs being a bad choice. But should someone go to jail for just doing drugs? That is the reality of what is happening. I believe the time has come for that to end.

I've been talking about legalization and not decriminalization. Legalization means we educate, regulate, tax, and control the estimated $400 billion a year drug industry. That's larger than the automobile industry. Decriminalization is a muddy term. It turns its back to half the problems involved in getting the entire drug economy above the line. So that's why I talk about legalization, meaning control, the ability to tax, regulate, and educate.

> *Legalization means we educate, regulate, tax, and control the estimated $400 billion a year drug industry.*

We need to make drugs controlled substances just like alcohol. Perhaps we ought to let the government regulate them; let the government grow or manufacture, distribute and market them. If that doesn't lead to decreased drug use, I don't know what would!

Kids will tell you that legal prescription drugs are harder to come by than illegal drugs. Well, of course. To get legal drugs, you must walk into a pharmacy and show identification. It's the difference between a controlled substance and an illegal substance. A teenager will tell you that a bottle of beer is harder to come by than a joint. That's where we've come. It's where we've come to with regard to controlling alcohol, but it shows how out of control drugs have become.

Losing the war on drugs

Drug Czar Barry McCaffrey has made me his poster child for drug legalization. He claims that drug use has been cut in half and that we are winning the drug war. Well, let's assume that we have cut it in half. I don't buy that for a minute, but let's assume that it's true. Consider these facts: In the late 1970s the federal government spent a billion dollars annually on the drug war. Today, the feds are spending $19 billion a year on it. In the late 1970s, we were arresting a few hundred thousand people. Today, we're arresting 1.6 million. Does that mean if drug use declines by half from today's levels, we'll spend $38 billion federally and arrest 3.2 million people annually? I mean, to follow that logic, when we're left with a few hundred users nationwide, the entire gross national product will be devoted to drug-law enforcement!

Most people don't understand, as we New Mexicans do, that the mules are carrying the drugs in. I'm talking about Mexican citizens who are paid a couple hundred dollars to bring drugs across the border, and they don't even know who has given them the money. They just know that it's a king's ransom and that there are more than enough Mexican citizens willing to do it. The federal government is catching many of the mules and some of the kingpins. Let's not deny that. But those who are caught, those links out of the chain, don't make any difference in the overall war on drugs.

A teenager will tell you that a bottle of beer is harder to come by than a joint.

I want to tell you a little bit about the response to what I've been saying. Politically, this is a zero. For anybody holding office, for anybody who aspires to hold office, has held office, or has a job associated with politics, this is verboten. I am in the ground, and the dirt is being thrown on top of my coffin. But among the public, the response is overwhelming. In New Mexico, I am being approached rapid-fire by people saying "right on" to my statements regarding the war on drugs. To give an example, two elderly ladies came up to my table during dinner. They said, "We're teachers, and we think your school voucher idea sucks. But your position on the war on drugs . . . right on!"

What I have discovered, and it's been said before, is that the war on drugs is thousands of miles long, but it's only about a quarter-inch deep. I'm trying to communicate what I believe in this issue. Drugs are bad, but we need to stop arresting and locking up the entire country.

7

Drug Use Should Be an Individual Choice

Thomas Szasz

Thomas Szasz is a professor of psychiatry emeritus at Syracuse University in New York (SUNY) Health and Science Center. A Libertarian, Szasz is an advocate of individual rights and an annual civil liberties award has been created in his name. He is also the author of Our Right to Drugs: The Case for a Free Market.

Before the twentieth century, American citizens held the responsibility for their drug-using behavior. Since 1914, however, that responsibility has been transferred to the state. Although some supporters of the legalization of marijuana argue that the use of marijuana can be medically beneficial, this philosophy encourages the idea that drug use is an appropriate object of government control. In a free society, the decision to use drugs belongs to the individual.

Drug prohibitionists were alarmed in November 1996, when voters in Arizona and California endorsed the initiatives permitting the use of marijuana for "medical purposes." Opponents of drug prohibition ought to be even more alarmed: The advocates of medical marijuana have embraced a tactic that retards the repeal of drug prohibition and reinforces the moral legitimacy of prevailing drug policies. Instead of steadfastly maintaining that the War on Drugs is an intrinsically evil enterprise, the reformers propose replacing legal sanctions with medical tutelage, a principle destined to further expand the medical control of everyday behavior.

Not surprisingly, the drug prohibition establishment reacted to the passage of the marijuana initiatives as the Vatican might react to an outbreak of heretical schism. Senator Orrin G. Hatch, chairman of the Senate Judiciary Committee, declared: "We can't let this go without a response." Arizona Senator Jon Kyl told the Judiciary Committee: "I am extraordinarily embarrassed," adding that he believed most Arizona voters who supported the initiative "were deceived." Naturally. Only a person who had fallen into error could approve of sin. Too many critics of the War on

Drugs continue to refuse to recognize that their adversaries are priests waging a holy war on Satanic chemicals, not statesmen who respect the people and whose sole aim is to give them access to the best possible information concerning the benefits and risks of biologically active substances.

Transferring responsibility to the state

From Colonial times until 1914, Americans were the authors of their own drug policy: they decided what substances to avoid or use, controlled the drug-using behavior of their children, and assumed responsibility for their personal conduct. Since 1914, the control of, and responsibility for, drug use—by adults as well as children—has been gradually transferred from citizens to agents of the state, principally physicians.

Supporters of the marijuana initiatives portray their policies as acts of compassion "to help the chronically or terminally ill." James E. Copple, president of Community Anti-Drug Coalitions of America, counters: "They are using the AIDS victims and terminally ill as props to promote the use of marijuana." He is right. Former Surgeon General Jocelyn Elders declares: "I think that we can really legalize marijuana." If by "legalizing" she means repealing marijuana prohibition, then she does not know what she is talking about. We have sunk so low in the War on Drugs that, at present, legalizing marijuana in the United States is about as practical as is legalizing Scotch in Saudi Arabia. A 1995 Gallup Poll found that 85 percent of the respondents opposed legalizing illicit drugs.

> *It is not the government's business to protect individuals from harming themselves.*

Supporters of the marijuana initiatives are posturing as advocates of medical "responsibility" toward "sick patients." Physicians complain of being deprived of their right to free speech. It won't work. The government can out-responsible the doctors any day. Physicians have "prescription privileges," a euphemism for what is, in effect, the power to issue patients *ad hoc* licenses to buy certain drugs. This makes doctors major players in the state apparatus denying people their right to drugs, thereby denying them the option of responsible drug use and abdicating their own responsibilities to the government: "We will not turn a blind eye toward our responsibility," declared Attorney General Janet Reno at a news conference on December 30, 1996, where the Administration announced "that doctors in California and Arizona who ordered for their patients any drugs like marijuana . . . could lose their prescription privileges and even face criminal charges." I don't blame the doctors for wanting to forget the Satanic pact they have forged with the state, but they should not expect the government not to remind them of it.

A medicalized view of life

The American people as well as their elected representatives support the War on Drugs. The mainstream media addresses the subject in a language that precludes rational debate: crimes related to drug prohibition are systematically described as "drug-related." Perhaps most important, Americans in ever-increasing numbers seem to be deeply, almost religiously, committed to a medicalized view of life. Thus, Dennis Peron, the originator of the California marijuana proposition, believes that since relieving stress is beneficial to health, "any adult who uses marijuana does so for medical reasons." Similarly, Ethan Nadelmann, director of the Lindesmith Center (the George Soros think tank for drug policy), states: "The next step is toward arguing for a more rational drug policy," such as distributing hypodermic needles and increasing access to methadone for heroin addicts. These self-declared opponents of the War on Drugs are blind to the fatal compromise entailed in their use of the phrase "rational policy."

If we believe we have a right to a free press, we do not seek a rational book policy or reading policy; on the contrary, we would call such a policy "censorship" and a denial of our First Amendment rights.

If we believe we have a right to freedom of religion, we do not seek a rational belief policy or religion policy; on the contrary, we would call such a policy "religious persecution" and a denial of the constitutionally mandated separation of church and state.

So long as we do not believe in freedom of, and responsibility for, drug use, we cannot mount an effective opposition to medical-statist drug controls. In a free society, the duty of the government is to protect individuals from others who might harm them; it is not the government's business to protect individuals from harming themselves. Misranking these governmental functions precludes the possibility of repealing our drug laws. Presciently, C.S. Lewis warned against yielding to the temptations of medical tutelage: "Of all the tyrannies a tyranny sincerely exercised for the good of its victims may be the most oppressive. . . . To be 'cured' against one's will and cured of states which we may not regard as disease is to be put on a level with those who have not yet reached the age of reason or those who never will; to be classed with infants, imbeciles, and domestic animals."

Although at present we cannot serve the cause of liberty by repealing the drug laws, we can betray that cause by supporting the fiction that self-medication is a disease, prohibiting it is a public health measure, and punishing it is a treatment.

8

Legalization of Drugs Is Sound Economic Policy

Walter Block

Walter Block is professor and chair of the Department of Economics and Finance at the University of Central Arkansas, in Conway, Arkansas. Block is a recognized authority on issues of the free market and a Libertarian. Block has published many articles on drug legalization and public policy.

A free market in drugs enhances economic welfare, and economic principles do not support the arguments against legalization. In economic terms, those who are not directly involved in a drug transaction should have no input; in a free society, addicts should be allowed to choose whether or not they are better off with or without drugs. Although legalization would not solve all problems with drugs, it could be no worse than the present situation, in which the government cannot even control drug use in its own prisons. The public health argument against legalization fails because prohibition does not improve, but exacerbates the health problem: Smugglers, balancing risk and profit, choose to smuggle more potent drugs. Some argue that because narcotics and opiates have been illegal for nearly a century, most people do not believe they have a right to use narcotics. This argument is irrelevant in a free society where people have the right to use drugs, whether they know that or not.

This paper argues the case for legalizing[1] drugs such as marijuana, cocaine and heroin. It claims there are no market failures that justify prohibiting of these opiates, and there is nothing in positive economics that precludes legalizing drugs. On the contrary, a free market in marijuana and other drugs enhances economic welfare.[2]

This conclusion stems from the argument that there are always gains from trade. Whenever any two persons engage in commercial activity both must gain in the *ex ante* sense since neither party would take part in the endeavour unless he expected to be made better off from it.

The claim is not that a free market in drugs will enhance economic

Reprinted from Walter Block, "Drug Prohibition and Individual Virtue," *Review of Political Economy*, November 4, 1996. Available at www.tandf.co.uk/journals. Reprinted with permission from Taylor & Francis Ltd.

welfare *ex post,* but only in the *ex ante* sense. When viewing trade *ex ante,* one does so before it actually takes place and anticipates a benefit from it. That is the reason one agrees to take part in it. Economic welfare in the *ex post* sense occurs after the trade. To have gained in this regard the participant must continue to regard himself as better off because of the trade.

If this insight applies to ordinary trades, it holds no less in the case under consideration. Were I to sell you an ounce of cocaine for $100, at the point of sale I must value the money more than the opiate. and you must rank the two items in the inverse order. Since trade is a positive sum game, we both gain.

It cannot be denied that third parties often feel aggrieved. Citizens may be affronted when consenting adults engage in voluntary capitalist acts, temperance leagues might object to alcohol sales, and health advocates might object to cigarette advertising. But as third parties their misgivings do not count in welfare calculations.

A free market in marijuana and other drugs enhances economic welfare.

There are several good reasons for disregarding the welfare of third parties.[3] First, according to the old saw, 'talk is cheap'. A third party can verbally oppose any given trade. But that opposition cannot be revealed through market choices in the same way that trade between the two parties indicates a positive evaluation of the transaction.

Secondly, by definition, third parties do not take part in market transactions, and no benefit accrues to them on those occasions. People, of course, are free to enter the market and offer goods or services for trade. Only then can their economic welfare be enhanced. But the welfare of third parties *qua* third parties cannot be counted, since we do not contend it will be enhanced.

Several objections might be raised against these claims.[4]

Drug-related problems

After citing statistics on the large number of drug-related problems it is frequently argued that things would not improve with legalization.

One reply to this might be 'So what?' No one ever claimed that legalization would solve *all* problems. If legalization makes drug-related problems no worse, and improves matters in other ways, there would be a prima facie case for ending prohibition.

Legalization will likely reduce drug-related problems. Impurities in narcotics would be better dealt with by legitimate businesses than the present fly-by-night operations created by prohibition. And there would certainly be fewer drive-by shootings, which indiscriminately kill innocent bystanders.

The implication of this objection appears to be that if drugs were prohibited the problems would dissolve. But there are serious difficulties with this line of reasoning. First, since drugs like crack are already outlawed, the horrible statistics indict the present system, not the non-existent legalization scenario. Secondly, it is widely conceded that government cannot successfully ban addictive substances from its own jails where, presumably, bureaucrats have more control than elsewhere in society. But if the state cannot prohibit opiate use in prison, it is unlikely to eradicate drug use outside prisons without resorting to policies that circumscribe civil rights.

Coercion

According to B. Steinbock:

> If one is forced to trade ('Your money or your life'), then one does not gain, even in the *ex ante* sense. How does this relate to the sale of narcotics? Some drugs, such as crack cocaine, are highly addictive. The choices of addicts are not fully voluntary, perhaps not voluntary at all. They are constrained, comparable to the 'choice' of a person who has a gun to his head.

This objection is problematic because one can gain by choosing even under the threat 'Your money or your life'. If you value your life more than your money, you are better off if you are allowed to choose life over money. Consider an addict offered one ounce of his favourite narcotic for $100. Are we to say that he would be better off, from his own perspective, if he could not make this choice? If the person in danger of being murdered is made better off by being given a choice, why does this not apply to the addict?

The 'public health' perspective

According to this viewpoint, addictive materials are physically harmful to the person who uses them and they should be banned, even though others are not harmed. Drug prohibition is viewed here as analogous to seat belt laws which save thousands of lives each year. As Steinbock argues: 'Since the infringement on individual freedom is minuscule, and the social good so great, the intrusion is warranted'.

But such inherently unquantifiable variables cannot be measured, much less weighed against each other. Interpersonal comparison of utility is incompatible with valid economic analysis.

If legalization makes drug-related problems no worse, and improves matters in other ways, there would be a prima facie case for ending prohibition.

Moreover, many things besides drugs and driving without seat belts are deleterious—chocolate, ice cream, hang gliding, boxing, automobile racing, and fried chicken to name a few. Were we to accept the logic of the public health argument we would have to forbid all these items and activities.

Let us concede for the sake of argument that heroin is harmful. Even so, legal suppression does not improve the health problem; rather it exacerbates it. This is because the more severely prohibition is administered, the stronger will be the potency of the ensuing drugs. A smuggler would rather risk transporting a suitcase full of cocaine than marijuana because of its greater value. In the early 20th century prohibition led beer manufacture to decline and hard liquor manufacture to increase.

Many people might become addicted under legalization

There are good reasons to suppose that the number of addicts would not rise significantly by ending prohibition. Drugs are a necessity, not a luxury. to users; and the price elasticity of demand should be very low. Under legalization, incentives to 'hook' an addict would be reduced.

Moreover, even if, say, three-quarters of the population were to become addicts. there would still be nothing in positive economics to justify banning these substances themselves. Again, many of the disastrous effects of narcotics stem not from the actual substances, but from their prohibition. Under legalization, the usual social problems associated with drugs (crime, overdosing, the frantic attempt to find a fix) would tend to disappear.

Since drugs like crack are already outlawed, the horrible statistics indict the present system, not the non-existent legalization scenario.

Suppose that were homosexuality legally prohibited 1% of the population would engage in this practice. Alternatively, were it allowed, 75% of males would engage in it. Would Professor Steinbock advocate forbidding homosexuality under such assumptions? Suppose further that under prohibition the spread of AIDS would be very much decreased. Would her 'public health approach' then urge a law incarcerating gays?

Yes, libertarianism "has absurd results," as Steinbock maintains. But this is due to our absurd supposition of 75% addiction—made only for argument's sake. When equally unlikely assumptions are fashioned so as to attack other philosophies, they, too, can be shown to be "absurd," based on such a faulty criterion.

Alcohol prohibition and the argument from the status quo

According to Steinbock: 'Because narcotic and opiate drugs have been illegal since the beginning of this century, they aren't viewed by most people as something to which they have a right. *Keeping* drugs illegal would not engender widespread anger and resentment, as *making* alcohol illegal would.'

Missing from this analysis is any concern with liberty or freedom. Such concern would lead us to ask not whether people think they have a right to some substance but whether they actually do have these rights. Concern with liberty would lead us to ignore political feasibility.

Consider a doctor who recommended in the 1950s that people stop smoking in order to save themselves from cancer. At that time, tobacco use was very well entrenched; perhaps even more than alcohol at present. Given the political impossibility of changing the smoking habits of Americans in the 1950s, Steinbock would have thrown up her hands in dismay and given up the good fight. A person with a true concern with public health, in contrast, would have said: 'I don't care whether it is politically possible or not, tobacco causes cancer. Case closed. Full steam ahead, and let's ban cigarettes!'.

But there is yet another problem with this argument about feasibility—according to the logic of the argument we should have never prohibited narcotics at the turn of the century, nor should we have prohibited alcohol in the 1930s. For these policies, at those times, would have led to 'widespread anger and resentment'.

Notes

1. Actually relegalization, since these substances were legal until the passage of the Harrison Narcotics Act in 1914.

2. For a general discussion of drug prohibition see Judson 1974; Trebach 1978; Szasz 1985; Hamowy 1987; Boaz 1990; Thornton 1991.

3. We are here discussing third parties whose rights to person and property are not being violated.

4. These objections have been articulated by Steinbock (1994) in response to Block (1994).

9

The Dangers of Marijuana Use Are Exaggerated

Ethan A. Nadelmann

Ethan A. Nadelmann is the director of the Lindesmith Center, a drug policy and research institute created to inform the public debate on drug policy. Nadelmann is a critic and commentator on United States and international drug control policies, and his writings on drug policy have appeared in a number of periodicals, including the National Review, Rolling Stone, *and* American Heritage.

Those who are fighting the war against marijuana use scare tactics to oppose legalization of pot. Although marijuana is dangerous if used irresponsibly, most who have used marijuana have not been permanently harmed. Yet the government discourages research that might not support its stand against marijuana. Research shows that increased potency of marijuana does not increase its danger, and no evidence proves that marijuana influences sexual development or permanently damages memory or other cognitive functions. Moreover, the "gateway theory" which suggests marijuana leads to more dangerous drugs has no basis in fact.

"The war on drugs is really a war on marijuana," says professor Lynn Zimmer, a sociologist at Queens College, in New York, who is widely regarded as one of the nation's leading analysts of drug policy. Marijuana, says Zimmer, is the leading justification for drug testing in the workplace, the main target of anti-drug efforts in the schools and the media, and the principal preoccupation of drug warriors in and out of government today. The drug warriors' tactics include—along with arrests, seizures, incarceration and the intimidation of doctors who would prescribe pot for the terminally ill—a more sinister approach. Spokesmen are quoted by journalists and appear on the evening news and on talk shows, making frightening claims about marijuana's harmful effects, spinning unproven theories and, in some cases, distorting the known truth in an effort to demonize even casual users of pot.

It's no wonder that the warriors find themselves in a quandary. They're essentially fighting a war against the 70 million Americans who have tried marijuana, including half of all Americans aged 18–35 and more than a quarter of everyone older than 35. Polls have indicated that a fourth of all adult Americans favor legalizing pot, which, after alcohol, tobacco and caffeine, is the fourth most popular psychoactive drug in the world.

"You can't scare middle-class parents with a war on heroin and cocaine," says Zimmer. "These drugs are too removed, too remote. Marijuana brings it home."

There is ample evidence that the majority of the 70 million Americans who have tried marijuana are doing just fine.

Bill Clinton's administration, desperate not to appear soft on drugs, has indulged in its share of scare tactics. Clinton's newly appointed drug czar, General Barry McCaffrey, has set the tone for the federal government's new stance, threatening sanctions against medical doctors in California and Arizona (RS 750/751), where citizens voted in November 1996 to allow the medicinal use of cannabis. More typical, however, is the approach taken by [former] Secretary of Health and Human Services Donna Shalala, who disingenuously told reporters in December 1996, "All available research has concluded that marijuana is dangerous to our health."

The research on marijuana use

Is pot dangerous? Is there any scientific research to back up Shalala's claim? There are, of course, reasons to be concerned about marijuana. It is, like alcohol, a powerful psychoactive drug. Used irresponsibly, it contributes to accidents on the roads and in the workplace. During the period of intoxication, short-term memory is impaired. Heavy pot smokers face some of the same risks as cigarette smokers. And some people become dependent upon marijuana, using it as a crutch to avoid dealing with relationships and responsibilities.

Among kids, especially, it is the daily use of marijuana, not experimental or occasional use, that merits concern. According to the latest annual survey of drug use among high-school students, the percentage of eighth-graders who admit to daily pot smoking increased from 0.2 percent in 1991 to 1.5 percent in 1996. Among 10th-graders, there was an increase from 0.8 percent to 3.5 percent; among seniors, an increase from 2 percent to nearly 5 percent. Of course, smoking marijuana every day would contribute to a teenager's problems in school and socially, but more likely it is an indicator of something else that is basically wrong.

On the other hand, there is ample evidence that the majority of the 70 million Americans who have tried marijuana are doing just fine. Since the early 1970s, the government has funded studies that have ended up proving that pot is not harmful, then disavowed the findings. In 1988, following an extensive review of the scientific evidence on marijuana, the Drug Enforcement Administration's own administrative-law judge, Francis Young, concluded that marijuana "in its natural form is one of the safest therapeutically active substances known to man." Virtually every independent commission assigned to examine the evidence on marijuana and marijuana policy—including the Shafer Commission appointed by President Richard Nixon, a National Academy of Sciences committee in the early 1980s, and numerous others both in the U.S. and abroad—have concluded that marijuana poses fewer dangers to individuals and society than either alcohol or tobacco and should be decriminalized.

And there is little reason to expect anything different from the Clinton administration's January 1997 announcement that it will spend $1 million to review all the evidence on the medical benefits of marijuana. The problem is that no Congress or president has ever had the guts to follow through on the recommendations of independent commissions assigned to balance the risks and harms of marijuana with the risks and harms of marijuana policies. It's still impossible, for instance, for any government official to speak out publicly about the difference between responsible and irresponsible use of marijuana, as they would with alcohol. All marijuana use is defined as drug abuse—notwithstanding extensive evidence that most marijuana users suffer little if any harm. That position may be intellectually and scientifically indefensible, but those in government regard it as politically and legally obligatory.

The claims against marijuana

So the government resorts to scare tactics and misinformation, relying increasingly on three claims: that today's marijuana is much more potent than the version that kids' parents smoked a decade or two ago; that new research has shown the drug to be more dangerous to our health than previously thought; and that marijuana use is a gateway to more dangerous drugs.

Are these claims true? Is today's marijuana much more potent? Is marijuana much more dangerous than previously believed? Is marijuana a "gateway drug"?

It's impossible for any government official to speak out publicly about the difference between responsible and irresponsible use of marijuana.

Most marijuana researchers depend on government grants to finance their studies. This poses two problems. First, the government tends to encourage and fund only those research proposals that seek to identify harmful effects of marijuana. There are few incentives to investigate the benefits of marijuana, medicinal or otherwise, and little interest in determining either the safety margins of occasional use or ways of reducing the harms of marijuana use. Studies that identify marijuana as harmful are well publicized by the governments' public-affairs officers. Findings that fail to confirm any harms are ignored.

Second, few marijuana researchers dare publicly challenge the government's anti-marijuana campaign. Scientists know that the grant-review process can be both scientifically objective and politically subjective. If too many studies fail to identify and emphasize the harms of marijuana, subsequent research proposals may not fare well in grant competitions. It takes a lot of courage for a scientist—dependent upon government grants for his or her livelihood—to raise questions about government policies and statements regarding marijuana. Not many scientists are that brave.

It is impossible to consume a lethal dose of marijuana, regardless of its THC content.

Fortunately, there are a few researchers who maintain their independence. Zimmer, the sociologist at Queens College, and Dr. John P. Morgan, a physician and pharmacologist who teaches at the City University Medical School, in New York, don't rely on government funding. They have completed a book, *Marijuana Myths, Marijuana Facts: A Review of the Scientific Evidence*, that systematically analyzes and dissects hundreds of studies on marijuana, including virtually all of those cited by government officials and other anti-drug crusaders to justify the war on marijuana. The result is the most comprehensive and objective review of the scientific evidence on marijuana since the National Institute of Medicine's report in 1982—one that both debunks many of the myths propagated by drug warriors and tells the truth about what is actually known of marijuana's harms and margins of safety. What follows is drawn largely from their work.

The potency question

No claim has taken hold so well as the charge that marijuana is much more potent than in the past. "If people . . . confessing to marijuana use in the late '60s . . . sucked in on one of today's marijuana cigarettes, they'd fall down backward," said William Bennett, President George Bush's first drug czar, in 1990. "Marijuana is 40 times more potent today . . . than 10, 15, 20 years ago," another drug czar, Lee Brown, claimed, in 1995. And from the ranking Democrat of the Senate Judiciary Committee, Joseph Biden, in 1996: "It's like comparing buckshot in a shotgun shell to a laser-guided missile."

Is any of this true? No. Although high-potency marijuana may be more available today than previously, the pharmacological experience of smoking marijuana today is the same as in the 1960s and 1970s. The only data on marijuana potency over time comes from the government-funded Potency Monitoring Project at the University of Mississippi. Since 1981, the average THC (tetrahydrocannabinol, marijuana's principal psychoactive chemical) content of PMP samples—all of which come from drug seizures by U.S. police agencies—has fluctuated between 2.28 percent and 3.82 percent. The project's findings during the 1970s were substantially lower, possibly because the samples were improperly stored (which can cause degradation of THC) and partly due to an overdependence on low-grade Mexican "kilobricks." Independent analyses of marijuana during the 1970s, which included samples from sources other than police agencies, reported much higher THC levels, ranging from 2 percent to 5 percent, with some samples as high as 14 percent.

Marijuana of less than 0.5 percent potency has almost no psychoactivity; in fact, in laboratory studies, subjects are often unable to distinguish a placebo from marijuana with less than 1 percent THC. It's not very likely that marijuana would have become so popular during the 1970s if the average THC content had been so low. Today, some regular marijuana users may have access to expensive, high-potency marijuana, often grown indoors under artificial light by small-scale, low-volume growers. But the potency of the "commercial grade" marijuana smoked by most Americans is not much different than it was 10, 15 or 20 years ago.

Even if marijuana potency had increased, that would not mean the drug has necessarily become more dangerous. It is impossible to consume a lethal dose of marijuana, regardless of its THC content. And in laboratory studies, smokers often fail to distinguish variations in potency of up to 100 percent. Increases of 200 percent to 300 percent in potency result in only 35 percent to 40 percent increases in smokers' "subjective high" ratings. "Bad trips" and other adverse psychoactive reactions typically have little to do with marijuana potency. Moreover, when potency increases, smokers tend to smoke less, thus causing less damage to their lungs.

The bottom line is this: If parents want to know what their kids are smoking today, they need only recall their own experiences. Neither marijuana nor the experience of smoking marijuana has changed much.

Sex, health and memory

Claims of increased THC potency aside, much of the new war on marijuana relies on claims of new scientific research that shows marijuana to be far more dangerous than previously thought.

There are tons of anecdotal reports that marijuana enhances sex. And there are repeated claims that marijuana interferes with male and female sex hormones, can cause infertility, and produces feminine characteristics in males and masculine characteristics in females. Speaking at Framingham High School, in Massachusetts, in late 1994, President Clinton spoke about "the danger of using marijuana, especially to young women, and what might happen to their child-bearing capacity in the future."

What's the truth? Some animal studies indicate that high doses of THC diminish the production of some sex hormones and may impair reproduction. In human studies, however, scientists typically find no impact on sex-hormone levels. In the few studies that do show some impact, such as lower sperm counts and sperm motility, the effects are modest, temporary and of no apparent consequence for reproductive capacity. A real-life example: Jamaica's Rastafarians, who smoke large amounts of the sacred herb, appear to have no problem making babies.

In 1972, a letter to the *New England Journal of Medicine* described three cases of breast enlargement in men who had smoked marijuana. In 1980, a letter to the *Journal of Pediatrics* described a 16-year-old marijuana smoker who had failed to progress to puberty. Both reports received substantial publicity, but neither has been confirmed through research. But studies involving larger numbers of marijuana users and non-users have found no evidence that marijuana distorts or delays sexual development, masculinizes females or feminizes males. There may be good reasons for telling kids not to smoke marijuana, but the president's warnings were based on myth, not fact.

Now that thousands of people with AIDS are smoking marijuana to stimulate their appetites and promote weight gain, opponents keep insisting that marijuana's damaging effects on the immune system negate any potential benefits. Here again, the claims are based almost entirely on studies in which laboratory animals are given extremely large doses of THC. There's no evidence that marijuana users have higher rates of infectious disease than non-users. That's not to say that there are no dangers. For people with compromised immune systems, smoking can cause lung infections. There is also a risk for AIDS patients that they will contract a pulmonary disease called aspergillosis caused by fungal spores sometimes found on improperly stored marijuana. One solution to this problem would be careful screening of marijuana supplies, a role for the government or pharmaceutical companies. And that is another reason to prescribe legal, controlled marijuana to more than the eight Americans who are now entitled to receive it.

Everyone knows that marijuana—like other psychoactive drugs consumed in sufficient doses—screws up short-term memory. Kids who get high (or drunk) before going to class are less likely to learn what their teachers are trying to teach them. Their minds are more likely to wander. People under the influence of marijuana can remember things they learned previously, but their capacity to learn and recall new information is diminished. Although some find marijuana useful for problem solving and creative tasks, there is little question that marijuana is not conducive to learning in school and other highly structured environments.

There is no pharmacological basis for the gateway theory.

The question of whether marijuana use permanently impairs memory and other cognitive functions is a separate issue. During the '70s, the U.S. government funded three comprehensive field studies in Jamaica, Greece and Costa Rica, in which long-term heavy cannabis users and non-users were subjected to a battery of standardized tests of their cognitive functions. The researchers found virtually no differences between the two groups.

More recently, two studies funded by the National Institute on Drug Abuse reported evidence of cognitive harm in high-dose marijuana users. The first, published in *Psychopharmacology*, in 1993, found that heavy marijuana users—who reported seven or more uses per week for an average of 6.5 years—scored lower than non-users on math and verbal tests. But the researchers also found that "intermediate" users—those smoking marijuana five to six times per week—were indistinguishable from non-users.

The second study, published in the *Journal of the American Medical Association*, in 1996, found differences between daily marijuana users and those who smoked fewer than 10 times per month, but the differences were minor. The light smokers performed slightly better on two memory tests and one card-sorting test—while no differences were found on tests of attention, verbal fluency and complex drawing.

What we know now, based on existing research, is that if heavy marijuana use produces cognitive impairment, it is relatively minor—and may have little or no practical significance.

The gateway theory

The "gateway theory," formerly known as the "steppingstone hypothesis," has long been a staple of anti-marijuana campaigns. Marijuana use, it is claimed, leads inexorably to the use of more dangerous drugs like cocaine, heroin and LSD. If we can stop kids from trying marijuana, we can win the drug war.

The most recent, and oft-repeated, version of the gateway theory—an analysis conducted by the National Center on Addiction and Substance Abuse at Columbia University—asserts that youthful marijuana users are 85 times more likely than non-users to use cocaine. To obtain this figure, the proportion of marijuana users who had ever tried cocaine (17 percent) was divided by the proportion of cocaine users who had never used marijuana (0.2 percent). The "risk factor" is large not because so many marijuana users experiment with cocaine—only a minority actually do—but because people who use cocaine, a relatively unpopular drug, are likely to have also used the more popular drug marijuana. Similarly, marijuana users are more likely than non-users to have had previous experience with legal drugs like alcohol, tobacco and caffeine.

Alcohol, tobacco and caffeine do not cause people to use marijuana. And marijuana does not cause people to use cocaine, heroin or LSD. There is no pharmacological basis for the gateway theory, since marijuana does not change brain chemistry in a way that causes drug-seeking, drug-taking behavior. In fact, there is no theory here at all—just a description of the typical sequence in which people who use many drugs begin by using ones that are more common.

The relationship between marijuana use and the use of other drugs is constantly changing. In some societies, marijuana use follows, rather than precedes, use of heroin and other drugs. Among American high-school seniors, the proportion of marijuana users who have tried cocaine decreased from a high of 33 percent, in 1986, to 14 percent, in 1995. Americans who smoke pot may be more likely to try other illegal drugs than those who don't smoke it. But for a large majority of marijuana users, marijuana is a terminus rather than a gateway drug.

"Now we're putting the research into the hands of parents," Donna Shalala claimed at a recent press conference, renewing the government's war against marijuana. But if it's the truth that Shalala wants to distribute, Zimmer and Morgan's *Marijuana Myths, Marijuana Facts* is a better source.

10

Medicinal Use of Marijuana Should Be Permitted

William E. Stempsey

William E. Stempsey is a Jesuit priest and a medical doctor who teaches the philosophy of medicine and medical ethics at the College of the Holy Cross in Worcester, Massachusetts.

Marijuana relieves the pain, nausea, and vomiting that accompany the advanced stages of many illnesses and should be legalized for medicinal use. Although some who oppose medicinal use of marijuana argue that marijuana is an unproven drug, but relief of pain is difficult to quantify. What is more important is the fact that terminally ill patients have obtained relief from pain by using marijuana. The evidence used to support the argument that marijuana is a gateway to other drugs is also inconclusive. The federal government should not interfere with the war against pain and suffering that patients and physicians are fighting.

In the fall of 1997, *The New York Times* reported a memorial reading of the work of the leading Beat Generation poet, Allen Ginsberg. The meeting was interrupted by Johann Moore, the head of the New York City Medical Marijuana Buyer's Club, who announced, "I'm here to talk about the medical use of marijuana, which is what I want to talk about all the time." Later Mr. Moore said, "I figured I'd 'fess up right from the start that, despite a degree in literature, I've never read a line of his poems. I just figured the cultural milieu of a Ginsberg crowd would be receptive to my message."

I feel a bit like Mr. Moore. Opponents of the war on drugs will be receptive to my message. My point, however, is not to argue that the war on drugs has failed and ought to be abandoned, but rather that the ideology of the war on drugs has led to a Federal policy that makes it unlawful for physicians to prescribe a drug that has great potential to relieve the suffering of a large and diverse group of people.

Within weeks after voters in Arizona and California in 1996 approved propositions allowing physicians to prescribe marijuana for medical rea-

Reprinted from William E. Stempsey, "The Battle for Medical Marijuana in the War on Drugs," *America*, April 11, 1998. Reprinted with permission from *America*.

sons, President Bill Clinton, Donna E. Shalala, the Secretary of Health and Human Services and Janet Reno, the Attorney General, all condemned these propositions and promised loss of prescribing privileges and even prosecution for physicians who prescribed marijuana. The ideology, which the medical ethicist George Annas has dubbed "reefer madness," has led the Federal Government to formulate a policy based on bad reasoning. The argument for that policy goes this way: Marijuana is an illegal drug; no one should use any illegal drug for any reason; therefore no one should use marijuana for any reason. This argument against the legalization of the medical use of marijuana is just bad logic.

The medical uses of marijuana

The advanced stages of many illnesses are often accompanied by horrible side effects: intractable pain, nausea and vomiting. Smoking marijuana has brought relief to thousands of people suffering from these side effects. Indeed, marijuana has been so effective in many cases that people have been willing to risk imprisonment in order to obtain this relief.

Marijuana, like any drug, is not harmless. Probably the most dangerous effect of smoking marijuana is potential lung damage. This is because marijuana cigarettes contain very high levels of tar—about twice as much as tobacco cigarettes. It is true that users of this product will generally not smoke as much marijuana as tobacco smokers smoke tobacco, but the dangers of tar inhalation remain.

This should not be a great concern, however, for patients with terminal cancer or AIDS. People with glaucoma might also be willing to risk some potential harm to their health for the sake of preserving their sight. In fact, compared with the chemotherapeutic agents responsible for the nausea and vomiting that leads people to marijuana, marijuana itself is quite safe. According to testimony given to the Drug Enforcement Agency, one would have to consume 20,000 to 40,000 times as much marijuana as is contained in one marijuana cigarette—that is to say, nearly 1,500 pounds of marijuana in about 15 minutes—in order to ingest a fatal amount. The chemotherapy agents themselves are far more lethal.

The failure of arguments against legalization

Three arguments have been raised against the medical use of marijuana. First, it is said that marijuana is a drug of unproven safety and effectiveness, and such unproven drugs should not be allowed. But the effectiveness of medical marijuana has been attested to by thousands of patients who have used it illegally. Should it matter whether the relief of nausea and pain is the result of some "scientifically proven" direct chemical action of marijuana or is the result of a marijuana-induced euphoria? Pain and relief are notoriously difficult to quantify in controlled experiments. What counts is whether the suffering of a seriously ill patient is relieved, rather than whether or not data "prove" efficacy. Dronabinol, a drug that contains tetrahydrocannabinol, one of the active ingredients in marijuana, has been available by prescription for over 10 years. It is not widely used, however, because it is so difficult to measure an effective therapeutic dosage. Self-administered marijuana, on the other hand, has allowed patients a degree of control over the dosage and has proved quite effective.

The Food and Drug Administration has been much more flexible in the past, especially in the context of the AIDS epidemic. It has allowed individual patients to buy and use drugs not yet approved but under investigation, arguing that terminally ill patients have nothing to lose and should not be deprived of hope. The unproven-effectiveness argument against the medical use of marijuana is based not on science but on political ideology.

It should also be noted that physicians are allowed by law to prescribe narcotic drugs such as morphine for the relief of pain. With morphine, however, the difference between the dose that relieves pain and the dose that hastens death is very small. With marijuana, there simply is no risk of death.

A second argument against legalizing marijuana by prescription is based on the contention that legalization will inevitably lead to a substantial diversion of marijuana to the general public for sale and personal use. But the availability of drugs on the streets is not a function of the availability of prescription drugs. Morphine and other narcotics are available at present only by prescription, and there is no widespread abuse of these drugs.

In the third place, it is said that marijuana is a gateway to other, more serious drug abuse and that legalizing medical marijuana would send children the wrong message. A 1994 survey reported in The New York Times did find that 17 percent of current marijuana users said they had tried cocaine, and only 0.2 percent of those who had not used marijuana had tried cocaine. But, as George Annas points out, there are two ways to interpret this. One way is to conclude that those who smoke marijuana are 85 times as likely as others to try cocaine; another way is to conclude that 83 percent of pot smokers, that is five out of six, never try cocaine. As for sending the wrong message to children, Ellen Goodman, a Boston Globe columnist, asks a good question: "What is the infamous signal being sent to [children] . . . if you hurry up and get cancer, you, too, can get high?"

A federal prohibition against the prescription of a relatively safe and effective drug is an unfair intrusion into the doctor-patient relationship. Even the American Medical Association has called for the legalization of marijuana for medical use. Confronted by the growing opposition of physicians to this ban, the Federal Government issued a clarification of its policy. In essence, this statement said that physicians may discuss marijuana with their patients so long as they do not recommend its use. But it is a doctor's job to recommend the most effective therapies. Jerome Kassirer, M.D., the editor of the prestigious New England Journal of Medicine, is right when he calls the Federal policy prohibiting marijuana for medical use "misguided, heavy-handed and inhumane." The Federal Government does have a battle plan for its war on drugs, but that is not the war seriously ill people and their physicians are fighting. Physicians as well as their patients who suffer from the effects of devastating illnesses such as cancer and AIDS need proper armaments for their war on suffering. Marijuana may be just what the doctor should order.

11

Marijuana Should Not Be Legalized

Bob Barr

Bob Barr, a former U.S. attorney, is currently a U.S. Representative from the seventh district of Georgia who serves on the House Judiciary Committee.

The notion of legalizing marijuana as medicine is a tactic used by marijuana advocates to make marijuana and other drugs widely and legally available. Although no research proves smoking marijuana has any therapeutic value, evidence has revealed the dangers of marijuana use. Not only does marijuana contain carcinogens, impair memory, and lead to use of other drugs, the cost of marijuana's use in the workplace and on the roadways has been substantial. Moreover, the legalization of marijuana for medicinal purposes would lead to perverse interpretations of the law.

Eleven years ago, as the Reagan presidency and its successful "Just Say No" campaign were coming to a close, drug legalization advocates decided it was time for a change in tactics. With drug abuse rates actually dropping for the first time since the drug revolution began, and a White House strongly committed to fighting mind-altering drugs, the legalization movement faced a choice: become irrelevant, or camouflage its true goals in order to move its agenda forward. The movement chose for its disguise "Medical" marijuana.

The legalization strategy

As University of California at Los Angeles (UCLA) Public Policy Professor Mark Kleiman told the *New York Times* this month, "[m]edical marijuana was chosen as a wedge issue several years ago by people who wanted to move drug policy in a softer direction."

In other words, the true aim of medicinal marijuana advocates is not to put drugs in the hands of doctors and pharmacists. Rather, the goal is to make marijuana and other drugs widely and legally available. To them,

Reprinted from Bob Barr, "Marijuana Should Not Be Legalized, Under Any Pretense," *The Commonwealth*, June 1999. Reprinted with permission from Congressman Barr.

the medicinal-use argument is simply a contrived means to an end, using terminally ill patients as pawns in a cynical political game.

From a purely political standpoint, the medicinal strategy has worked rather well for the legalizers. Backed by a handful of wealthy patrons like George Soros, [an international investor and philanthropist], in a few short years legalization advocates have transformed themselves from socially unacceptable pariahs into the darlings of the national media. News reports on marijuana protestors at rallies became magically changed—with a speed that would make Cinderella green with envy—into stories about a repressive government denying "life-saving" drugs to "patients."

Putting the intellectual dishonesty of the legalization movement aside for a moment, let's take a look at the medicinal use argument on its own merits, or lack thereof.

Tetrahydrocannabinol (THC), the active ingredient in smoked marijuana, has been a legal prescription drug (marinol) available in the United States since 1984. For over a decade, physicians have been able to prescribe the active ingredient in marijuana. However, they rarely do, because other remedies—including drugs as well as medically-supervised pain management techniques—provide its therapeutic qualities more effectively. No reputable study has arrived at the conclusion that smoked marijuana has any therapeutic value sufficient to justify its medicinal use.

The dangers of marijuana

Not only is there no real proof that marijuana has any significant medicinal value, there is voluminous evidence that it is demonstrably harmful; if not deadly. For example, marijuana smoke contains roughly 30 times as many carcinogens as cigarette smoke. It is also dangerously addictive. Nationally, an estimated 100,000 individuals are in treatment for marijuana use.

Furthermore, inhalation of marijuana smoke depresses the immune system. This makes it likely that allowing its use by those with weak immune systems, such as Acquired Immune Deficiency Syndrome (AIDS) patients, would be highly questionable at best, and harmful at worst. Surely, well-informed observers would condemn a movement that fills the terminally ill with false hope, and encourages patients already vulnerable to pulmonary infections and tumors like Kaposi's sarcoma, to put a deadly substance in their lungs.

Moreover, marijuana use adversely affects the user's memory, a fact patently obvious in debates involving heavy marijuana users.

Marijuana use poses an even greater danger from a sociological standpoint than it does to the health of individuals who smoke it. Numerous studies have indicated marijuana use leads to abuse of other drugs like heroin, d-Lysergic Acid Diethylamide (LSD), and cocaine. Using data compiled by the Centers for Disease Control, researchers at Columbia University—hardly a bastion of conservative thought—concluded that children who drank, smoked cigarettes, or used marijuana at least once in the past month, were 16 times as likely to use another drug like cocaine, heroin, or LSD.

At the workplace, marijuana is a proven cause of absenteeism, accidents, and increased insurance claims. Estimates put the annual cost of on the job drug use at more than $100 billion per year.

On America's roads, marijuana poses a threat to all of us. Unlike alcohol, it is difficult to use roadside tests to determine the extent to which a driver is under the influence of marijuana, and there is practically no way for law enforcement to determine to what degree a particular driver's perception is altered by the drug, though by definition perception is altered (marijuana is a *mind-altering drug* for that reason). A recent study of reckless drivers found that 45% of those drivers not under the influence of alcohol tested positive for marijuana.

California has made national headlines by embarking on an obsessive campaign to eradicate cigarette smoking from public places. Ironically, in the same period, the state voted in favor of widely distributing a substance 30 times deadlier. What an imminently logical approach. What's next? Legalizing DDT and banning fly-swatters?

The effects of medicinal legalization

Proponents of allowing doctors to dispense marijuana frequently make the simplistic, but media-friendly argument that doctors, not the government, should decide what drugs to prescribe. Accepting this premise, why have an FDA approval process at all? Why not just return to the 19th century, when "doctors" could prescribe any remedy—from powdered rhinoceros horn to sugar water in medicine bottles—that they personally felt was efficacious? Who needs science? Why not just ignore science, shut down the FDA, get rid of pharmacists, and stock pharmacy shelves by voter referendum?

Where else would medicinal legalization lead us? Undoubtedly, high school students—backed by the American Civil Liberties Union (ACLU)—would begin filing and winning lawsuits for permission to smoke their "medicine" in class, under a perverse interpretation of the equal protection clause of the Constitution. Others, from prisoners to bus drivers, would assuredly do the same.

Medicinal use would create a nightmare for employers. Accidents would increase, and employers could no longer test workers for drug use, for fear of winding up in court. Adding insult to injury, companies would be forced to pay for workers to get stoned on the job by including marijuana "treatment" in health plans. Everyone who drives a car would also be forced to foot the bill for this folly, in the form of increased accidents and higher insurance rates.

The bottom line is that legalization advocates don't care about any of these things. They are motivated either by a simple desire to smoke dope because it makes them feel good, or a misguided political philosophy that tells them legalizing drugs would end crime with one magical puff of smoke.

Unfortunately, citizens of several states have been all too eager to buy the snake oil legalizers are selling, because it is tantalizingly packaged in fake compassion and false hope for the sick. Hopefully, voters in other states will take the time to carefully consider the facts before they make an ill-formed decision to follow California's example.

Organizations to Contact

The editors have compiled the following list of organizations concerned with the issues debated in this book. The descriptions are derived from materials provided by the organizations. All have publications or information available for interested readers. The list was compiled on the date of publication of the present volume; names, addresses, phone and fax numbers, and e-mail/Internet addresses may change. Be aware that many organizations take several weeks or longer to respond to inquiries, so allow as much time as possible.

Center on Addiction and Substance Abuse (CASA) at Columbia University
152 West 57th St., New York, NY 10019
(212) 841-5230 • fax: (212) 965-0465
e-mail: mnakashi@casacolumbia.org • website: www.casacolumbia.org

CASA is a think tank composed of professionals from many disciplines, including business, communications, medicine, sociology, law, and law enforcement whose goal is to inform Americans of the economic and social costs of substance abuse. The organization performs studies on gateway drugs, legalization, and the impact of substance abuse. CASA publishes articles including "Legalization: Panacea or Pandora's Box?"

Common Sense for Drug Policy
3220 N St. NW, Suite 141,Washington, DC 20007
(703) 354-5694 • fax: (703) 354-5695
e-mail: info@csdp.org • website: www.csdp.org

The goal of Common Sense for Drug Policy is to educate the public about alternatives to current drug policy by disseminating research, hosting public forums, and informing the media. Common Sense provides advice and technical assistance to allied organizations working to reform current policy and provides pro bono legal assistance to those adversely affected by current drug policy. On its website, Common Sense provides access to data and findings prepared by the American Civil Liberties Union, the Office of National Drug Control Policy, the Government Accounting Office, and the Bureau of Justice Statistics. The organization publishes a semiannual newspaper *Common Sense* and a book of facts and citations related to the war on drugs, *Drug War Facts.*

Drug Enforcement Administration (DEA)
Information Services Section (CPI)
700 Army Navy Dr., Arlington, VA 22202
website: www.usdoj.gov/dea

Part of the U.S. Department of Justice, the role of the DEA is to enforce the controlled substance laws and regulations of the United States, to bring to justice those involved in the growing, manufacture, or distribution of controlled substances, and to support nonenforcement programs aimed at reducing the availability of controlled substances on the domestic and international markets. On its website, the DEA provides the following DEA publications: "Drug

Legalization, Decriminalization and Harm Reduction," "Say It Straight: The Medical Myths of Marijuana," and "Speaking Out Against Drug Legalization."

Drug Sense/Media Awareness Project
PO Box 651, Porterville, CA 93258
(800) 266-5759
e-mail: greer@drugsense.org • website: www.drugsense.org

Drug Sense believes that prohibition creates illegal drug markets with unintended, but devastating side effects and is committed to heightening awareness of the damage caused by the "War on Drugs" by informing the public of rational alternatives to the drug war and helping organize citizens to bring about needed reforms. The organization provides online and technical support to reform organizations and information for research relevant to drug policy, maintaining a database of current news and opinion articles that call attention to factual errors and the excesses of policy. On its website, Drug Sense publishes an online newsletter, *Drug Sense Weekly Newsletter*, which features articles and news on current drug policy, and provides access to *The Drug Library*, which includes studies and government publications on drug policy, research on medical marijuana, and drug war statistics.

The Lindesmith Center Drug Policy Foundation (DPF)
4455 Connecticut Ave. NW, Suite B-500, Washington, DC 20008-2328
(202) 537-5005 • fax: (202) 537-3007
e-mail: dpf@dpf.org • website: www.dpf.org

The foundation believes that current drug policy is not working and supports alternatives to the war on drugs, including a shift away from criminal justice policies and a shift toward public health approaches to drug use and abuse. DPF provides grants for research on drug policy alternatives and hosts an International Conference on Drug Policy Reform. The organization publishes a twenty-four-page bimonthly newsletter, *The Drug Policy Letter,* and provides access to news articles that concern drug policy on its website.

The National Clearinghouse for Alcohol and Drug Information (NCADI)
Center for Substance Abuse Prevention
Substance Abuse and Mental Health Services Administration (SAMHSA)
U.S. Department of Health and Human Services
PO Box 2345, Rockville, MD 20847-2345
(800) 729-6686 • fax: (301) 468-6433
e-mail: info@health.org • website: www.health.org

NCADI is the information service of SAMHSA, providing a catalog of current information and material concerning substance abuse and drug policy. NCADI services include a staff that responds to inquiries, access to a prevention-related materials database, and distribution of brochures, pamphlets, posters, and videotapes available through its toll free number. The NCADI website, PREVLINE, provides access to the National Substance Abuse Web Index (NSAWI), which will search for legalization issues in documents, news releases, and links to related websites.

National Drug Prevention League (NDPL)
16 South Calvet St., Baltimore, MD 20202
(410) 385-9094 • fax: (410) 385-9096
e-mail: Augustus@erols.com • website: www.ndpl.org

NDPL believes that drug abuse and addiction are the root of the social, health, legal, and economic problems in the nation's families and communities. Its goal is to develop a national resolve against drug abuse by linking private drug abuse prevention organizations to promote public awareness, develop strategies and policy, and provide a national voice favoring drug abuse prevention. On its website, NDPL provides access to national surveys and studies, congressional bills, and fact sheets, including *1999 National Drug Control Strategy* and *1996 National Household Survey on Drug Abuse*.

National Institute on Drug Abuse (NIDA)
6001 Executive Blvd., Bethesda, MD 20892-9561
(301) 443-1124
e-mail: information@lists.nida.nih.gov • website: www.nida.nih.gov

Part of the National Institutes of Health, a research agency of the U.S. government, NIDA conducts research on how drug abuse affects the brain and behavior, transferring its data to policy makers, practitioners, and the general public. NIDA publications, available from the National Clearinghouse for Alcohol and Drug Information (NCADI) and the Government Printing Office (GPO), include *Drugs and Violence: Causes, Correlates, and Consequences, Economic Costs of Alcohol and Drug Abuse in the United States*, and *Needle Sharing Among Intravenous Drug Abusers: National and International Perspectives*. NIDA publishes a bimonthly newsletter, *NIDA Notes*, available from MasiMax Resources, Inc., 1375 Piccard Dr., Suite 175, Rockville, MD 20850.

National Organization for the Reform of Marijuana Laws (NORML)
1001 Connecticut Ave. NW, Suite 710, Washington, DC 20036
(202) 483-5500 • fax: (202) 483-0057
e-mail: norml@norml.org • website: www.norml.org

Since its founding in 1970, NORML has been the principal national advocate for ending the prohibition of marijuana. The organization provides information to media and lobbies state and federal legislators to permit the medical use of marijuana and to reject attempts to treat minor marijuana offenses more harshly. NORML publishes two quarterly publications, *NORML Legislative Bulletin* and *NORML Leaflet*. On its website, NORML provides access to studies, news releases, and the NORML newsletter.

Partnership for a Drug-Free America
405 Lexington Ave., 16th Floor, New York, NY 10174
(212) 922-1560
website: www.drugfreeamerica.org

Partnership for a Drug-Free America believes that changing attitudes toward drug use is the key to changing behavior, and the partnership's mission is to reduce demand for illegal drugs by making drug use less glamorous and less acceptable. On its website, *Drug-Free Resource Net*, the partnership provides access to fact sheets, press releases, bulletins, and studies, including the *Partnership Attitude Tracking Study*, which monitors the drug-related attitudes of children, teens, and parents. The partnership also publishes the monthly *Partnership Bulletin* and the biannual *Newsletter of the Partnership for a Drug-Free America*.

Bibliography

Books

Dan Baum	*Smoke and Mirrors: The War on Drugs and the Politics of Failure.* Boston: Little, Brown, 1996.
Eva Betram, ed.	*Drug War Politics: The Price of Denial.* Berkeley: University of California Press, 1996.
Robert H. Dowd	*The Enemy Is Us: How to Defeat Drug Abuse and End the "War on Drugs."* Miami: Hefty Press, 1997.
Dirk Chase Eldredge	*Ending the War on Drugs: A Solution for America.* Bridgehampton, NY: Bridge Works, 1998.
Jefferson M. Fish, ed.	*How to Legalize Drugs.* Northvale, NJ: Jason Aronson, 1998.
Erich Goode	*Between Politics and Reason: The Drug Legalization Debate.* New York: St. Martin's Press, 1997.
James A. Inciardi, ed.	*The Drug Legalization Debate.* Thousand Oaks, CA: Sage Publications, 1999.
Jill Jonnes	*Hep-Cats, Narcs, and Pipe Dreams: A History of America's Romance with Illegal Drugs.* New York: Scribner, 1996.
Janet E. Joy, Stanley J. Watson Jr., and John A. Benson Jr., eds.	*Marijuana and Medicine: Assessing the Science Base.* Washington, DC: National Academy Press, 1999.
Barry R. McCaffrey	*The Destructive Impact of Drugs on the United States: How Legalization of Drugs Would Jeopardize the Health and Safety of the American People and Our Nation.* Washington, DC: U.S. Office of National Drug Control Policy, 1999. Available from the U.S. Government Printing Office, Washington, DC 20401.
Marilyn McShane and Frank P. Williams II, eds.	*Drug Use and Drug Policy.* New York: Garland, 1997.
Richard Lawrence Miller	*Drug Warriors and Their Prey: From Police Power to Police State.* Westport, CT: Praeger, 1996.
Mikki Norris, Chris Conrad, and Virginia Resner	*Shattered Lives: Portraits from America's Drug War.* El Cerrito, CA: Creative Xpressions, 1998.
Jeffrey A. Schaler	*Drugs: Should We Legalize, Decriminalize, or Deregulate?* Amherst, NY: Prometheus Books, 1998.

Periodicals

Tom Bethell	"Drug Story," *American Spectator*, September 1995.
David Boaz	"Drug Legalization, Criminalization, and Harm Reduction," *Cato Institute*, June 16, 1999. Available from 1000 Massachusetts Ave. NW, Washington, DC 20001-5403.
Richard Brookhiser	"Lost in the Weed," *U.S. News & World Report*, January 13, 1997.
Lee P. Brown	"Why the United States Will Never Legalize Drugs," *Vital Speeches of the Day*, August 1, 1995.
Gordon Browne	"Time to Stake Out a Middle Ground in the Drug War," *Alcoholism & Drug Abuse Weekly*, November 25, 1996. Available from Manisses Communications Group, 208 Governor St., Providence, RI 02906.
William F. Buckley Jr. and Ethan A. Nadelmann	"The War on Drugs Is Lost," *National Review*, February 12, 1996.
Joseph A. Califano Jr.	"Fictions and Facts About Drug Legalization," *America*, March 16, 1996.
Dirk Chase Eldredge and Bill McCollum	"Would Legalizing Drugs Serve America's National Interest?" *Insight on the News*, September 14, 1998. Available from Insight on the News, 3600 New York Ave. NE, Washington, DC 20002.
Sarah Ferguson	"The Battle for Medical Marijuana," *Nation*, January 6, 1997.
David France	"Does This Woman Deserve to Be Locked Up for 24 Years?" *Glamour*, June 1999.
Jennifer Gonnerman	"The Politics of Pot," *Village Voice*, January 15, 1997. Available from 36 Cooper Square, New York, NY 10003.
Morton A. Kaplan	"The Drug Dilemma," *World & I*, January 1995. Available from World & I, 3600 New York Ave. NE, Washington, DC 20002.
Joseph D. McNamara	"Drug Peace–Legalization Research," *Vital Speeches of the Day*, November 1, 1999.
P.J. O'Rourke	"My Problem with the War on Drugs," *Rolling Stone*, January 20, 2000.
Ryan H. Sager	"Grass Roots," *National Review*, November 8, 1999.
Davis Sheremata	"Peace Looms in the War on Pot," *Alberta Report*, August 18, 1997. Available from United Western Communications Ltd., 17327 106A Ave., Edmonton, Alberta, T5S 1M7 Canada.
Richard Smith	"The War on Drugs," *British Medical Journal*, December 23, 1995. Available from BMJ Publishing Group, BMA House, Tavistock Square, London WC1H 9JR United Kingdom.
Jaime Vasconcelos	"Legalize It," *Mother Jones*, March/April 2000.
Eric A. Voth	"America's Longest War," *World & I*, February 2000.

Index

78